A Penguin Special
Television Today and Tomorrow

Christopher Dunkley was born in Scarborough and grew up in Hamp-stead, London. He was educated at Haberdashers' Aske's on a scholar-ship, where he edited the school magazine and helped start a national school magazine, *Sixth Form Opinion*. He toured Germany with a school production of *King Lear*, coxed the school first eight and was eventually expelled for being a 'persistently subversive influence'. He worked as a flyman at the Golders Green Hippodrome, a hospital porter at Paddington General and a cook at El Serrano before joining the *Slough Observer* in 1963 to work successively as a general reporter, cinema and theatre critic and shows page editor. Following that he became news editor and feature writer on the *UK Press Gazette* until 1968, when he joined *The Times* as night reporter, becoming first a general reporter, then Fleet Street's first mass media correspondent and also television critic. Since 1973 he has been television critic for the *Financial Times*. He has been a regular radio broadcaster since 1963, contributing to, among others, *Critics' Forum*, *Kaleidoscope* and *Meridian*, and an occasional television presenter, his series including *Edition*, *Real Time* and *Whistle Blowers*. In 1984 he wrote and presented an edition of BBC's *Panorama* called 'The Television Revolution'. Christopher Dunkley was named Critic of the Year in the British Press Awards of 1976. He lives in Kentish Town with his wife, Carolyn, his son, Damian, and his daughter, Holly. This is his first book.

D1362741

Television Today and Tomorrow
Wall-to-Wall Dallas?

CHRISTOPHER DUNKLEY

PENGUIN BOOKS

Penguin Books Ltd, Harmondsworth, Middlesex, England
Viking Penguin Inc., 40 West 23rd Street, New York, New York 10010, U.S.A.
Penguin Books Australia Ltd, Ringwood, Victoria, Australia
Penguin Books Canada Ltd, 2801 John Street, Markham, Ontario, Canada L3R 1B4
Penguin Books (N.Z.) Ltd, 182–190 Wairau Road, Auckland 10, New Zealand

Published in Penguin Books 1985
Copyright © Christopher Dunkley, 1985
All rights reserved

Made and printed in Great Britain by
Richard Clay (The Chaucer Press) Ltd, Bungay, Suffolk
Filmset in Monophoto Sabon by
Northumberland Press Ltd, Gateshead, Tyne and Wear

To my parents,
Robert and Joyce Dunkley

Contents

Acknowledgements

I wish to thank my wife, Carolyn, who not only did her own job as well as keeping the family sane, well fed, laundered, and delivered to all the right places as usual, thus enabling me to write this book, but also typed the entire manuscript once and most of it twice.

I am also grateful to Geoffrey Owen, editor of the *Financial Times*, for running one of the few civilized newspapers remaining in Fleet Street. Had he not allowed me to take a virtually instant sabbatical the book would not have been written.

Louise Medawar generously put her entire photocopying department at my disposal, a kindness which I exploited shamelessly; and Melvyn Bragg, one of the busiest people I know, readily found time to read the manuscript, making precisely the sort of suggestions for improvements which I had expected, and saving me from howlers. Any which remain are my responsibility alone.

C.D.

List of Abbreviations

ABC	American Broadcasting Company
ATV	Associated Television
BAFTA	British Academy of Film & Television Arts
BARB	Broadcasters' Audience Research Board
BBC	British Broadcasting Corporation (from 1922 to 1927 British Broadcasting Company)
BT	British Telecom
C4	Channel 4
CBC	Canadian Broadcasting Corporation
CBS	Columbia Broadcasting System (USA)
CND	Campaign for Nuclear Disarmament
CNN	Cable News Network
CTV	Canadian Television
DBS	Direct Broadcast Satellite/Direct Broadcasting by Satellite
D-G	Director-General
ECS	European Communications Satellite
HBO	Home Box Office (US cable network)
HDTV	High Definition Television
HTV	Harlech Television

IBA	Independent Broadcasting Authority
ITA	Independent Television Authority (from 1954 to 1972, thereafter IBA)
ITAP	Information Technology Advisory Panel
ITN	Independent Television News
ITV	Independent Television
JPM	Jolts per minute
LWT	London Weekend Television
MEAL	Media Expenditure Analysis Ltd
NARAL	Net Advertising Revenue After Levy
NBC	National Broadcasting Company (USA)
PBS	Public Broadcasting Service (USA)
PCG	Programme Controllers' Group (UK)
RAI	Radiotelevisione Italiana
RCA	Radio Corporation of America
SBB	Satellite Broadcasting Board
SMATV	Satellite Master Antenna Television
TAM	Television Audience Measurement
TSW	Television South West (UK)
TVE	Television Trust For The Environment
TVS	Television South (UK)
TW3	That Was The Week That Was
VCR	Videocassette Recorder
WTBS	Call sign of Ted Turner's American 'SuperStation'

CHAPTER ONE

Old Prophecies, New Processes

Making predictions about the mass media is a chancy business. D. W. Griffith, the director of such famous silent movies as *Birth of a Nation* and *Intolerance*, said: 'I believe that a hundred years hence the airplane passenger lines will operate motion picture shows on regular schedules between New York and Chicago and New York and London.' He was speaking in 1925, thus predicting that this marvel would come about in 2025.

In his 1935 pamphlet *What To Do with the BBC* Raymond Postgate declared that 'Television will only become a home amusement in homes that have several rooms. Not more than 10 per cent of the population will take it up permanently.'

In 1948 when Grace Wyndham Goldie moved from radio to television Bertrand Russell told her: 'My dear girl it will be of no importance in your lifetime or mine.'

In 1971 Professor Emmanuel G. Mesthene of Harvard University said: 'I would not want to count on the quick advent of wired cities – even if the cable technology exists – in the face of youth who display a taste for the simple life and communal living.'

In 1976 the IBA (Independent Broadcasting Authority) told Lord Annan's committee on broadcasting that video recorders would appeal to 'only the minority that is acutely choosy in its attitude to broadcasting and can afford the equipment which makes it possible to be choosy'.

Griffith's prediction came true of course but he was quite wrong in guessing how long we would have to wait for in-flight movies.

Postgate was proved even more hopelessly inaccurate. Television's global audience by 1985 was 2.5 billion in 162 countries. In Britain 98 per cent of households had acquired television sets (84 per cent colour) and nearly 50 per cent had two or more. Furthermore British viewers watched an average of four to five hours television a day (less in summer but even more in winter: thirty-eight hours four minutes in Christmas week 1984) which is still two hours a day less than their American counterparts and a long way from Japanese figures which show an astonishing eight hours a day average. Nevertheless the British now spend more time in front of the box than in any other activities except sleeping and working – and if the trend continues, viewing will soon overtake working.

Russell too was profoundly wrong. Within nine years of her move to television Grace Wyndham Goldie was heading the department which launched the *Tonight* programme. That in turn launched the television careers of Alasdair Milne (Director-General of the BBC), Alan Whicker, Julian Pettifer, Cliff Michelmore and many others. In 1962 *Tonight* gave birth to *That Was The Week That Was* so that Mrs Goldie was also responsible in a sense for starting the television careers of David Frost and Bernard Levin.

Professor Mesthene's predictions were faulty on both counts: ten years after his pronouncement the student passion for communal living and the simple life had virtually evaporated but cable companies were scrambling over one another to wire up American cities. By 1984 there were some 5,700 cable television systems in the US, 2,000 of them with a capacity of twenty or more channels, and 34 million homes were taking cable services.

The IBA people were equally wide of the mark in their disdainful conclusions about video recorders. When they made their remarks about 'only the acutely choosy' buying such machines the cost was about £750, pre-recorded tapes were £150 to £250 for thirty to forty minutes, and blank tape cost £20 an hour. By the spring of 1985 you could buy a three-hour blank tape for £4.95, a pre-recorded film for about £25, and the machines themselves for as little as £350. At the start of 1985 VCRs were installed in more than 7 million UK homes, the highest penetration of any major country, and the expectation was that 10 million would be in use by 1988, meaning that 50 per cent of British homes would be equipped.

These examples are just a small sample of the mass-media predictions which have been confidently asserted during the past sixty years and proved wrong almost before the words had died away. At this stage in the history of television only the naïve or those desperate to create self-fulfilling prophecies would dare make dogmatic forecasts and this book is not one of those gee-whiz efforts in which the aim is to induce awe at the complexities of modern technology. It is more concerned with programmes than equipment – 'software' rather than 'hardware' in the jargon of the trade.

Yet there is no denying that it was the possibilities presented by new technology which led to the writing of the book in the first place. As in so many other areas of life it is advances in technology rather than changes in social or political needs which appear to have caused most changes in television in the past and it seems likely that this will continue to be so in the future. Thanks to technological advances in the last twenty-five years we are faced today with the prospect of greater changes than at any time in the fifty-year history of television. The difficulty with considering television in the nineteen-eighties and nineties lies not in discovering potential futuristic marvels but in deciding which of the bewildering array of possibilities are likely to become realities in Britain, though some television people believe they know what is going to happen and that it will mean the biggest disaster ever inflicted upon broadcasting.

Whether we like it or not, the type of technology which is introduced may to some extent, perhaps a large extent, decide the sort of programmes made available. For example, there would be little chance of establishing a movie channel in a country which decided to stick exclusively to the type of airborne broadcasting which is so familiar to us in Britain; there are simply not enough wavelengths. On the other hand the most advanced technology –

direct broadcasting by satellite (DBS) – could make it very difficult for governments to control what their citizens see: it would need totalitarian control of the hardware to prevent viewers gaining access to whatever programmes they fancied. In order to stop people mounting satellite receiver dishes on their homes and pulling out of the sky Rupert Murdoch's light entertainment or Ted Turner's American news, governments would have to use the sort of controls currently employed by Soviet Russia to prevent its citizens laying their hands on photocopying machines (wide access to which could turn the cottage industry of samizdat literature into a major business). The difference, of course, is that whereas photocopiers are bulky, expensive and complicated, the domestic satellite dish is relatively small, cheap and simple.

At the very least the technologies which are chosen, or permitted, will inevitably have some effect upon the range of choices available to us, and it therefore seems right to begin with a description of the more important new technologies now waiting in the wings. Everything in the following list exists already somewhere in the world, and in many cases there are prototypes already in the UK though that is no guarantee that we shall all be using them soon. 'Videophone' systems have been feasible for decades but the idea has never caught on, pay-TV was tested in Britain twenty years ago but never developed, and so on.

Cable TV

This is one of the two most important of the 'new' technologies (the other being the space satellite) since it is a delivery system which nullifies the old limitation on the possible number of television channels. That limitation was caused by the need to send signals through the air on wavelengths so scarce that they were rationed out, country by country, by international agreement. If obliged to stick to that old system of broadcasting airborne signals from high transmitter masts, used in the UK since 1936, it would be difficult for British television ever to offer viewers a choice of more than half a dozen channels in colour.

Cable systems of a sort have been in use virtually since the beginning of radio. In Britain they have been mostly buried or fixed to the front of terraced houses though the Americans tend to hang them from poles. They were laid originally in areas where off-air reception was poor for geographical reasons. The business started in the nineteen-twenties and thirties with radio and continued in the fifties in places where television reception was bad. However, these systems run by companies such as Rediffusion and Visionhire used old-fashioned cable which is unable to carry more than a few channels of television. The signals are delivered by wire in the manner of a telephone system.

Modern broadband copper-coaxial cable can carry dozens of channels, and if you use the most advanced fibre-optic cables with hair-thin glass strands instead of metal wire, combined with modern switching systems, the number of possible channels is virtually infinite. Most important of all perhaps, in the longer term, modern cable systems can be 'interactive': like telephones they allow the consumer not only to receive signals but to send signals back down the line. The possibilities of this are manifold, ranging from instant opinion polls (already tried in Britain's Granada TV area) and the ordering of food or wine (already possible through Britain's Homelink system which connects the telephone cable to the television), to telebanking, teleshopping, automatic meter-reading and burglar alarm systems (which are in experimental use in Milton Keynes).

Low-Power Satellites

The principle of the communications satellite was first expounded by Arthur C. Clarke, the man who went on to write *2001: A Space Odyssey*. In 1945, the year when V-2 rockets were landing on London, Clarke published an article in the magazine *Wireless World* pointing out that if a rocket could release a man-made satellite at exactly the right height above the earth (22,300 miles as it happens) its flight path ought to be such as to keep it at the same spot relative to the surface of the earth all the time, in 'geosynchronous orbit'. Such satellites could then be used to relay radio messages around the globe. Not only did his idea work for radio and consequently telephone signals, but also for television.

Today there are scores of satellites whirling around above the world like the chairs of a charaplane but without the connecting chains. A ground station provides the 'uplink' beaming signals to the satellite, which is fitted with a number of 'transponders', perhaps twenty-four, each capable of receiving, amplifying and retransmitting either one television signal or a thousand telephone calls at a time. The satellite can relay its signals over a wide area of the globe, its precise coverage, known as its 'footprint', depending upon its position in the sky. Such satellites can be used for sending signals from one country to another as with news programmes or Olympic Games coverage. However, they are used most heavily these days, notably in North America, in conjunction with cable operators to form nation-wide distribution systems capable of delivering clear pictures over vast distances in even the worst geographical conditions.

The channel producer – perhaps the USA's Home Box Office (HBO) which concentrates on movies, or Ted Turner's Cable News Network (CNN) which provides a non-stop news channel – sends its signal up to a transponder on, say, the Galaxy satellite which is owned and operated by Hughes Communications. Hughes paid $145 milion to put this particular 'bird' into orbit and sold eighteen of its transponders for $270 million before the rocket cleared the gantry. The satellite retransmits the HBO and CNN signals in a footprint covering most of the USA from New York to San Francisco, and local cable operators all over the country use satellite receiver dishes 10 to 20 feet across (3 to 6 metres) – they have to be that big to work with so-called 'low-power' satellites – aimed very carefully at Galaxy, to pick up the signal. It takes less than a quarter of a second for a signal to travel from the ground station up to the satellite, and back to a receiver dish. The local cable operators then feed HBO and CNN down the wires to all their customers who have paid for those particular services, or they may decide to provide a 'basic tier' of services – five to ten channels perhaps – for an all-in fee.

Direct Broadcast Satellites (DBS)

Though DBS satellites employ exactly the same principles as those described above, they transmit high-power instead of low-power signals so that the service they provide on the ground can be rather different. Low-power signals call for big receiver dishes, thus making it uneconomic for most individuals to own one, although driving along the Trans-Canada Highway today in areas where there is no cable television company you see as many 10-foot (3-metre) satellite dishes as dog kennels in front gardens; Canadians do like to be able to watch American television. With a high-power DBS signal, however, you only need a small dish-receiver which could easily be mounted in a back garden or on a roof, and possibly even inside a loft or indoors beside a window, so that most viewers might eventually be expected to have their own. By 1985 the size was down to that of an umbrella and the promise was that efficient 18-inch (45-cm) diameter models would soon be produced. It was generally accepted within the industry that the cost of a full DBS domestic receiving kit including a dish and the equipment needed to convert satellite signals into coherent pictures would need to be below £350 to buy or £15 a month to rent if DBS were to become popular enough to make it a going concern. The BBC, who took an early interest in DBS, have had their engineers working on a flat wall-mounted satellite receiver which would not only be smaller and neater than a dish but capable of 'tuning' from one satellite to another; a capability only offered at present by big and costly 'steerable' dishes.

DBS faces a chicken-or-egg problem: nobody wants to pay the millions of pounds needed to launch a satellite service unless they are pretty sure that they will quickly attract subscribers, yet there cannot be subscribers until domestic receiving kits are made available. But manufacturers are loath to tool up for the mass production of domestic receiving kits until they are sure that there will be a market for them, and they cannot be sure of that until the satellite is up – or, as they say in the business, until the bird flies. No bird, no egg; no egg, no bird.

SMATV

Master Antenna Television (MATV) was a system originally used in the USA by property developers who made their apartment blocks more desirable by mounting a single outsize aerial on the roof and running a cable to each flat to provide the tenants with good reception. Then when the US authorities de-regulated satellite dishes in 1979 one smart apartment dweller climbed up on the roof of his block, unhitched the aerial, mounted a $3,000 dish, and connected all the tenants direct to the sky thus creating Satellite Master Antenna Television: SMATV 'Smatvee'). Now the habit is becoming remarkably popular in the US where cable systems although widespread have failed to penetrate many of the major cities because companies bidding for local cable licences have met with unacceptable demands from the local authorities wanting access channels, local government channels, special phone links, interactive services and many other futuristic but expensive goodies. The cable companies take many of their services off satellite, and SMATV is a way for some urban dwellers in non-cabled cities to get the new satellite services before the cables are laid; instead of waiting for the cable company to get its licence, put up a dish and pipe the signal to them, they are simply cutting out the middle man and mounting their own dishes.

Now, thanks to the snail's-pace advance of cable in Britain, the same idea is being employed here, the intention being that satellite dishes could be mounted not only on blocks of flats but on hotels and pubs too. Those keenest on the idea are the entertainment companies which went into the business of supplying specialized TV services by satellite in expectation of cable customers only to find that there were practically no cable customers calling for their services; in particular Thorn EMI who found themselves running movie, rock music and children's channels expensively off the Intelsat V satellite to virtually nobody. Rupert Murdoch's Sky channel, a mixed entertainment service, runs off the ECS I satellite and has viewers scattered all over Europe and also a certain number in Britain linked to the 'upgraded' Rediffusion cable systems, but Sky could also be picked up by SMATV operators. Clearly the danger is that a keen uptake of SMATV facilities could kill the prospects for cable operation, and so the British Government has said that SMATV will only be permitted in areas where no cable franchise has been awarded. If SMATV was a huge success wherever it was permitted it could stop cable in its tracks outside the few areas already licensed, though that hardly seems likely.

Videodiscs

The great misfortune for the videodisc was that it arrived some time after the enormously successful videocassette system (featured in the next chapter) with the result that, so far, it has remained at the margin. For the domestic user the great drawback of the videodisc is that, like the LP, it does not permit home recording: the viewer who wants to record *Panorama* and watch it the next day cannot do so, all he can do is buy or hire pre-recorded material. It is cheaper to buy a movie on videodisc than on cassette (and personal experience suggests that the picture is less likely to deteriorate after repeated playing on videodisc than on cassette) but most people do not want to buy movies to keep, they are happy to hire overnight.

However, in three respects the videodisc system is superior to videocassettes: it provides 'instant access', perfect freeze-frame facilities, and superb sound. If you want to find a particular place on a videocassette you have to wind all the way through the tape, then, when you get near the right place, watch on 'fast forward' until you find the exact spot. The videodisc system, on the other hand, works like a record player only better and allows instant access to any part of the disc's surface. Furthermore it will, unlike VCRs, display a single frame perfectly for as long as you like. The great differences between record players and videodiscs are that LPs revolve at $33\frac{1}{3}$ rpm and are played by a diamond or sapphire stylus, and videodiscs spin at 1,800 rpm and are played by a laser so that there is no wear. In addition to being able to carry movies and other conventional programme material, videodiscs can also store up to 108,000 still frames per disc and display any one of them on demand, the instant the index number is keyed in. Consequently they make ideal video reference systems whether for do-it-yourself car mechanics or fine art catalogues. Furthermore, new equipment has brought them into the orbit of the personal computer, enabling the videodisc to be used as a vast data bank providing the computer with up to a billion characters of data per disc.

Though videodiscs are used increasingly in education and especially for industrial training, the system has suffered so far because it has been seen largely as a competitor for VCRs and, for domestic users, an inferior competitor. Once its extraordinary capacity as a data storage system becomes better known and more widely applicable it will surely sell not as an alternative to VCRs but as an adjunct to home computers.

HDTV

Among several ways of improving the performance of television in the home, 'high definition television' (HDTV) is the most promising. It produces a pin-sharp picture, as good as 35 mm film, by using 1,125 lines to form the television picture in place of the 625 lines currently used in Britain or the 525 lines used in the USA. Sony, Panasonic, Ikegami and CBS have all demonstrated HDTV, which was one of the attractions at Expo 85 at Tsukuba in Japan.

HDTV faces difficulties, however. First it cannot be received on existing sets, which are not only technically incompatible but the wrong shape: in place of the present squarish 4:3 aspect ratio, HDTV delivers a 5:3 picture, much closer to the wide-screen cinema shape, something like the proportions of a shoe-box lid. Secondly HDTV would require programme-makers to buy new cameras, new monitors, and new editing equipment. Thirdly the signal carrying HDTV takes up five times as much 'bandwidth' as the existing 625-line system making it virtually useless as a broadcast signal. It could, however, be tremendously tempting for DBS operators, particularly those specializing in movies, since it would deliver a splendid picture and customers gearing up for DBS would in any case be acquiring new equipment.

HDTV's sharp picture also makes it ideal for displaying print on screen, and the Japanese (who read even more newspapers per capita than the British but have even more trouble than the British in moving daily papers around their difficult terrain) see HDTV as an ideal medium for the electronic transmission of newspapers.

A British high definition system known as 'Enhanced C-MAC' has been developed by IBA engineers, and a third system by RCA. There is a danger that, as with the videocassette, three (or even more) incompatible systems will all come into use, creating tremendous difficulties between broadcasters internationally, and forcing viewers either to choose or to spend much more money.

Flat Screen TV

Sony and Sinclair both use so-called 'flat screen' technology instead of the bulky cathode ray tube in their miniature sets, the Sony 'Watchman' being $7\frac{3}{4} \times 3\frac{1}{2} \times 1\frac{1}{2}$ inches (19.5 × 9 × 4 cm) and the Sinclair 'Microvision' $5\frac{1}{2} \times 3 \times 1\frac{1}{4}$ inches (14 × 7.5 × 3 cm). Neither sold very well initially except, it is said, amongst American sports fans wanting to take them to baseball games in order to watch the slow-motion replays. Projected sales in Britain during the late eighties, however, are for 5 million sets a year. More important eventually than these miniature sets may be the full-size flat screen televisions of the sort demonstrated at Expo 85 by Matsushita. The manufacturers showed a 10-inch (25-cm) set just 4 inches (10 cm) deep, producing a distortion-free image over the entire screen, which they believe will form an ideal receiver for HDTV.

3-D and All That Jazz

There are all sorts of other improvements and innovations in the offing which may one day become popular or even standard equipment in every home, though in some cases it hardly seems likely. It is possible, for instance, that another Japanese prototype on exhibition at Expo 85, a 3-D system using signals from five cameras to produce a three-dimensional effect without the need for tinted spectacles, could one day spread world-wide, although commercial production was said to be years away.

'Large screen' television employing projection systems to produce pictures anywhere between 4 and 8 feet across (from 1.2 to 2.4 metres) are becoming increasingly popular in American homes and are available in Britain, but even in the US fewer than 200,000 were sold in 1984 compared to sales of 15 million conventional sets.

Televisions with hi-fi sound systems are becoming more popular, which can only be a good thing considering the appalling quality of sound from normal sets.

Stereo-sound sets are becoming more common with the growth of stereo videocassettes, a trend likely to increase with the introduction of cable or DBS since both will probably carry stereo signals.

And, following the hi-fi music craze for selecting and 'racking' individual items of equipment, television is now being sold in component parts: tuner, monitor, speakers and so on. The manufacturers claim that consumers will save by buying only one set of high-quality speakers, only one channel tuner instead of one each for television and VCR, and they say that we shall be able to add extra modules as new services come along. But since the first component system required an outlay of about £1,500 they seem unlikely to take over the mass market in a hurry.

CHAPTER TWO
VCR and JPM

The way in which habits may change to suit the new technology, rather than vice versa, and the way those changed habits may affect television is being made clear by our use of two pieces of relatively new equipment which are already proving popular: the videocassette recorder (VCR) and above all the seemingly insignificant remote control.

In the winter of 1982–3 Britain's tabloid press discovered that after years of fairly steady growth both in the size of television audiences and the average number of hours watched there had been a sudden dip in the graph. There is little love lost between the mass circulation newspapers and television since the sales and influence of the former have declined as the popularity and influence of the latter have risen, so with some glee the papers started asking 'What became of the missing millions?' It was suggested that the popularity of television had finally peaked and that viewers were simply switching off because programmes were so awful.

To a sceptic both suggestions sounded like wishful thinking and sure enough, within a couple of years, not only had audiences climbed back into huge figures but the average number of hours watched per capita was at its highest ever. What then caused the dip in the graph and the 'missing millions'? In part it may have been real; compared to the previous very successful season television was offering less attractive schedules and perhaps some people did watch slightly less for a while. In part it may have been due to new ways of calculating the ratings; the Broadcasters' Audience Research Board (BARB) was changing methods used for recording the activities of its viewing panel. But the further away we get from that period the more it looks as though the chief culprit was the videorecorder.

By the time the millions started to go 'missing' several million homes were fitted with VCRs. Most were not bought but rented for about £15 a month; they represented a new flow of trade for high-street TV rental companies whose business had been tapering off as the trade-up to colour television passed its peak.

A VCR is actually a television receiver and tuner with a built-in recording device but no screen. All it needs in order to show a picture is a slave monitor screen. When a home acquires a VCR the aerial is unplugged from the television set and plugged into the recorder, and a connector is run from the recorder to the TV set. It then becomes possible to do one of four things.

First you can operate the television normally watching a programme as it is transmitted, with the signal arriving via the aerial, running straight through the VCR and registering on the TV screen as usual. Under these circumstances BARB's measuring system counts you in the ratings, and provided you continue to use the tuner on the television set that continues to be so.

Secondly you can switch on the television and select the channel which is tuned in to your VCR; possibly channel 5 since channels 1 to 4 are usually tuned to BBC 1, BBC 2, ITV and Channel 4. You can then play a pre-recorded film rented from a video library or shop. Costs vary widely, with most dealers requiring an initial deposit and then charging between £1 and £3 for a film, though some UK Indians who have developed a voracious appetite for films in their own language are served by dealers who charge as little as 30p per film. Although the watching of pre-recorded films represents a low proportion of VCR use in Britain and is not therefore statistically very significant in terms of ratings, it was missed altogether from the

BARB figures until well into 1985 by which time some 20 million people had access to VCRs.

Thirdly you can switch the television on, select the channel which is tuned in to your VCR and then play back a programme you have previously recorded yourself. This habit known as 'time shifting' is much the most popular way of using a VCR. (Though experience suggests that people record far more than they ever find the time to watch; one programme is recorded over the top of another thus wiping the original recording before it has been seen.) This type of viewing which certainly is statistically significant was also being missed by BARB.

Fourthly you can switch on your television, select the channel tuned in to your VCR and watch off-air television via the receiving and tuning mechanism of your VCR. For those who have remote control systems for their VCR this makes sense because it means they can cover all operations (channel changing, starting and stopping recording, and playing back) with just one control box instead of two. This, however, was another mode in which BARB failed to count viewers.

Thus British viewers who had taken to home video-recording so soon and in such large numbers seem to have had quite a significant effect upon the ratings figures, and those figures are of more than passing interest to the people who run television; they are an important factor in deciding advertising rates and consequently have a direct effect upon the financing of the industry. By early 1985 the television trade press was starting to carry stories about the monster US broadcasting networks 'catching a cold', and one experienced British commentator reporting back on the 'mystery defection by American TV viewers' actually used the phrase 'missing millions'. But the reason for the apparent fall in American off-air viewing did not seem very hard to find: in 1983–4 the Americans had finally taken to the VCR and in the first half of that year bought 3 million machines. Projections were that many millions more would be sold in 1985 and 1986.

However, while VCRs have the gratifying effect of shifting power from broadcaster to viewer by giving the viewer the choice of when to watch and – to a much greater extent than ever before – what combination of programmes to watch (for instance ITV's nine o'clock programme followed at ten o'clock by BBC 2's nine o'clock programme from your own recording), all of which may put the cat among the ratings pigeons for a while, it is nevertheless the little arm-rest channel changer which is now seen by some in the industry as the bigger threat. To give viewers the power to flick from channel to channel effortlessly by remote control, 'zapping' as it is called, is to invite them to ignore the commercials. It is as though newspaper readers were to acquire gadgets able to select and destroy advertisements while retaining all the editorial columns.

Though most people may be too lazy to change channels merely for the duration of a commercial break if it means getting out of their chair and crossing the room, many will happily do so once it becomes a question of simply pushing a button on the control box on the arm of the chair. Advertisers keep fairly quiet about zapping, perhaps for fear of publicizing the practice, but they are becoming quite anxious about its effects not least because they have no clear idea of its incidence; audience measurement systems are not yet able to record zapping. However, advertisers are well aware that ownership of remote control is becoming widespread. By the spring of 1985 out of 30.5 million television sets in Britain 6.5 million were already equipped and with shops and high-street rental companies using the gadget as an inducement to trade up, half the new sets going into homes now have remote control.

Even more important in the long term is the effect of the remote control upon the arcane business of schedule building. A lot of rather pretentious terminology has been used to describe the techniques employed by broadcasters to construct schedules in such a way as to maximize audiences: 'inheritance factor' for instance, and 'pre-echo' and 'hammocking'. All they mean is the number of viewers handed on by one programme to the next (inheritance), the number of viewers a programme gains by people switching on early to be sure not to miss the start of the following programme (pre-echo), and the placing of high-rated programmes at either end of a less popular programme to give it support (hammocking). But in each case what it comes down to is the viewers' inertia: having watched a favourite show they cannot be bothered to get out of their chairs to change channels but stay for the next programme on the same channel (inheritance); rather than watch the end of *Name That Tune* on ITV which is what they fancy when taking their places in front of the set at 7.45 they switch on to Channel 4 straight away to be ready for *Brookside* at 8.00 and catch the whole of *Comment* because they do not want to have to get up again to change channels so soon after sitting down (pre-echo); and at the end of *Coronation Street* rather than get up and switch over to BBC 1 for half an hour and then get up again to switch back, they stay with ITV for *World in Action* because they want to see the drama which follows it (hammocking).

Yet on the day the remote control comes into the house all of that goes out of the window because the viewers know they can zap from channel to channel without having to move more than their index fingers. Worse still from the broadcaster's viewpoint, if the first half of *Brookside* seems a bit dull the viewer can, and does, use the commercial break to zap through the other channels from the comfort of the armchair, staying with anything which seems preferable. The more worried and hard-headed advertisers in the US are beginning to demand more JPM (jolts per minute) from the programmes they sponsor, to be as sure as possible of holding their viewers and keeping their fingers away from the remote control.

The advertisers' worries reach nightmare proportions, however, when contemplating the growing number of viewers possessing VCRs who timeshift their favourite programmes and play back using the remote control to zip straight past the commercials on the 'fast forward' button, a feature which allows you to run videotape at ten times the usual speed so that (on British television which insists upon an identifiable break) you can just distinguish where the commercials end and the programme begins. As the fast-forward habit grew during the mid eighties, makers of commercials were putting their heads together to try to create advertisements which maintained their impact even when viewed at ten times the normal speed. Such is the effect of just one small aspect of one technological innovation.

Throughout the first half of the eighties the British Government was planning hopefully, with considerably more hope than success in fact, for technological innovation on a scale which would make VCRs and remote controls look like gimcrack gewgaws. The technical possibilities of cable and satellite seem to have dazzled some of those in the upper reaches of the Conservative Party inspiring a passionate, some would say almost hysterical, response.

CHAPTER THREE
An Entertainment-Led Revolution?

It seems clear from their public pronouncements, and even clearer from some of their private ones, that Margaret Thatcher and certain Cabinet ministers (notably Kenneth Baker, former Minister for Information Technology) became convinced in about 1980 that the 'age of information' was just over the horizon. The belief was that if British businessmen could only be properly motivated they would set off at a sprint towards this apparition and start up some of the 'sunrise industries' which would ensure the arrival of the Information Revolution even sooner.

The most bullish of the believers maintain that this revolution will be more important than the Agrarian Revolution started by Britain in the eighteenth century or the Industrial Revolution led by Britain in the nineteenth century. A note of almost religious fervour creeps into their voices when they declare that late-twentieth-century Britain could be ideally placed to lead the world into yet another new era. They list Britain's advantages: a densely populated small country, blessed with mostly benevolent geography and climate, and a sophis-ticated citizenry which has already moved a remarkable way into the 'leisure age', taking to VCRs and home computers with greater enthusiasm than anyone else in the world. Better still, our engineers have a lot of advanced knowledge about the new generation of cable technology.

'Do you realize the implications of what's going on?' the believers ask, marvelling at the scope of their own vision. They describe how, once upon a time, most people lived in the country and worked on the land simply to produce the food needed to keep us all alive. Then the Agrarian and Industrial Revolutions changed everything and most people ended up living in cities and working in factories with only 5 per cent of the work-force left in the fields using modern methods and machinery to produce food for the whole population and for trade.

Now robots and computers are reducing the numbers working in smokestack industries, say the believers breathlessly (averting their eyes from such trivialities as the 1984–5 miners' strike), and soon manufacturing may also be employing as little as 5 per cent of the work-force. Then, just as food gave way to manufactured goods as the chief commodities of the economy, so in the post-industrial society manufactured goods will give way to information.

And how exactly does British television feature in this futuristic vision? Centrally. Some of the country's leading politicians earnestly believe that if only they move fast enough their legacy to posterity could be the world's first 'wired society'. By this they mean a society in which homes are linked to a nation-wide web of modern cables with interactive facilities.

In addition to the jobs that would be created in the construction, maintenance and supplying of such a network, they say, when it exists Britain will be able to use it as a springboard into a shiny new world of paperless offices, decentralized staffing (no need to 'go to work' and hang about the coffee machine when everyone is 'on line' to everyone else from the sitting-room) and a new role as the world's leading software exporters.

If we are quick enough, they declare, we could become hardware exporters too, building cable networks for other countries and spreading the Information Revolution round the world just as we previously built the world's railways to spread the Industrial Revolution – though even British politicians mostly realize now that the Americans and the Japanese are the more likely industrial imperialists of the electronic age.

With Postgate, Russell and Mesthene in mind it would take a brave and foolish forecaster to deny that some at least of this may happen one day. But what does it have to do with *Coronation Street*? The answer, perhaps surprisingly, is a tremendous amount thanks to the British Government's concept of an 'entertainment-led revolution', the idea being that in order to lure the public into this age of information you have to bribe them with the prospect of lots more telly.

In that unwieldy phrase – 'entertainment-led revolution' – the current fashionable political belief in market forces has met the current fashionable technological belief in 'convergence' and linked hands joyfully. The term 'convergence' is used to describe the way in which the once separate technologies of telephone, radio, broadcast television, computers, satellites and cable (not to mention film, television and videocassettes which 'converged' some time ago) are rapidly coming together to form an inextricably interwoven web of information and distribution, all leading ultimately to the television screen.

To the believers in market forces the notion of convergence came as a godsend since it pointed the way out of a terrible dilemma. The obvious way for a country to acquire a nation-wide network of interactive cable is for the government to finance it out of the public purse and for the national telephone company to construct it. Britain's telephone company, BT (British Telecom), has all the experience in cable-laying, all the existing ducts, and all the necessary wayleaves giving permission to dig up land and cross private property.

Better still, BT has some of the world's most advanced knowledge of cable switching systems and fibre-optics, those astounding bundles of hair's-breadth glass strands which can carry thousands of two-way signals, sound and vision, inside one little plastic-coated cable. BT could have given Britain the world's most modern interactive cable system either using fibre-optics throughout from the beginning or else laying configurations which would easily convert to fibre-optics later.

This approach would have ensured that we did not end up with radically varying and even incompatible systems built piecemeal around the larger urban areas, a foreseeable hazard when you permit the 'cherrypicking' habits of commercial cable operators who naturally prefer to select the choicest demographic morsels and ignore the hinterland. BT could have built a coast-to-coast system penetrating deep into the countryside, using cross-subsidization to finance the costly rural lines out of the more profitable urban systems, just as they always have with the telephone service.

Had the Thatcher administration of 1979 poured its enthusiasm for new technology into a scheme such as this then Britain might indeed have shown the world the way into the age of information. BT's nation-wide interactive service could have operated as a common-carrier network, like the road or telephone systems in principle, and anyone would have been able to pay to use it. Not only would it have carried business data and telephone traffic (the real money-spinners) and 'telebanking' and 'teleshopping' and all the other cable wonders, it would also have allowed the development of an infinite number of television 'broadcasters' – or 'narrowcasters'. Anyone with a video camera could have tried selling programmes; television would at last have become as universally available as print, with pamphleteers at one extreme 'publishing' single basic programmes and international conglomerates at the other extreme supplying entire libraries.

For those of us who admire the extraordinary achievements of British television to date but have grown impatient with its faults – its tedious occupation of what it claims is the middle ground, its abject fear of the erotic, its insistence on closing down and instructing us to turn off our sets just when some of us are waking up, its bias against independent programme-making, its insistence upon showing all the good things simultaneously so that you don't know what to watch and then all the rubbish simultaneously so that there isn't anything to watch, its pretence that religion is still central to the lives of most of us, its awe of politicians and its fawning upon royalty, in other words the insidiously paternalistic way in which it seeks to satisfy all the prejudices of its mass audience – for those of us who have grown tired of all that, the national broadband cable network might have been a dream come true.

Once the scarcity of wavelengths became an irrelevance, and cable arrived with its virtually limitless potential for diversity so that there was no longer any excuse for government licensing any more than there is in the print medium, then surely television could at last grow up and behave like the other adult mass media. Cable television could carry real politics with the gloves off just like *Militant* or the *Daily Telegraph*. It could carry programmes as sexually explicit as Ovid's *Amores*. It could even go all the way and allow humanists and rationalists to talk about morality just the way they do in sixth-form common rooms. After all, with the customer choosing what to watch and paying for it, the Grundyist belief that every transmission must be suitable for a timorous old woman of either sex who happens to switch on by mistake could safely be forgotten. Television would have joined newspapers and magazines in the sense that you would select and pay for what you wanted, and they could publish anything that would gain an audience, subject simply to the general law of the land.

The trouble is that in needing billions of pounds of public money for its construction (and there is no doubt that it would cost billions) and a public utility to organize it, the BT network plan reeks of *dirigisme* and is consequently anathema to free marketeers. Not only did Mrs Thatcher and her Government have no intention of spending a single penny of public taxes on cable TV, they were actually intent upon taking BT out of the public sector and privatizing it.

How, then, was Britain to acquire its cable network? Private enterprise of course. But what private company would ever risk the capital needed to cable the whole of Britain? None, so piecemeal licences would be offered area by area with encouragement for the licence-holders to wire up some of the hinterland as well as the choicest urban and suburban areas. And given that most people would almost certainly not want to pay a hefty monthly fee merely to receive BBC 1, BBC 2, ITV and C 4 off a wire instead of an aerial and would probably still not be tempted even if you threw in telebanking, teleshopping, and channels for ethnic minorities and local council meetings, how was this brave new service to be marketed?

Answer, lots of extra entertainment: entire channels for new and not quite so new movies; whole channels of sport or news or rock videos or health or even (if we followed the American example) soft pornography – although the Thatcher administration certainly didn't think much of that bit of freedom. This, surely, would tempt people to say yes when the salesman arrived on their doorstep with the news that the trunk cable would soon be laid in their street and that for £20 a month, merely four times the licence fee, which they would still have to pay, they could have this glittering array of entertainment on tap. Once into the home under the banner of 'more entertainment' the cable could tow all the other services and facilities behind it: banking, shopping, domestic work stations, computerized encyclopaedias, everything necessary for the paperless society and the new age of information. Hence 'the entertainment-led revolution'.

It was decided that there would have to be a cable authority, politicians having no intention of relinquishing control of any part of television until absolutely necessary, but for the health of the industry speed was thought to be of the essence. So in the summer of 1983, long before any sort of authority had been formed, the Government announced that up to twelve 'interim' franchises would be awarded later in the year and that, in order to provide an audience as quickly as possible for those planning to become programme suppliers for the cable business, operators of Britain's existing simple cable systems would be allowed to 'upgrade' immediately. Until 1983 Britain's cable services run by companies such as Rediffusion, Visionhire, Telefusion and Radio Rentals were virtually all limited to four-channel systems delivering BBC 1, BBC 2, ITV and C 4 to homes which, once upon a time, had suffered from poor off-air reception. But by 1983 the BBC/ITV transmitter systems practically everywhere had been so much improved that very few homes really needed cable delivery any longer. So the companies running these old services were told that provided they now supplied their customers with free roof aerials to receive BBC 1, BBC 2, ITV and C4 they would be allowed to sell any new services they could via their existing cable networks.

In autumn 1983 the Government announced that it had received thirty-seven applications for interim cable licences (the 'interim' being the period before the Cable Authority was set up) and that it was granting eleven. They were for Aberdeen, Belfast, Coventry, Croydon, Ealing, Glasgow (north), Guildford, Liverpool (south), Swindon, Westminster and Windsor. Then, almost as suddenly as it had started, the burst of cable activity stopped. The budget of March 1984 changed the rules about capital allowances in such a way that investors would no longer be able to offset cable-laying costs against profits from other holdings, a change which was seen by City investors as crucial. Aberdeen Cable Services, the only one of the eleven licence-holders actually to have started digging holes, promptly stopped and the other companies postponed their start dates. In June 1984 as a sop to the pioneers the Government agreed to extend operators' licences from twelve to fifteen years but refused to change the rules about capital allowances. In June 1984 Swindon Cable Services began laying new wire but Swindon was a special case: in 1973 it had been one of a small number of towns to experiment with local cable television and the need was now for enhancement rather than an entirely new system. The other interim licence-holders all hung back.

In August 1984 Richard Burton was named chairman of the Cable Authority. In September the Swindon company began operations with a handful of houses connected to the cable. In October it became known that Rediffusion and Visionhire were giving up their British cable operations. In November the other members of the Cable Authority were named and newspaper proprietor Robert Maxwell took a £2 million stake in Clyde Cable Vision. In December the Information Technology Advisory Panel (ITAP), whose enthusiastic

1982 report for the Cabinet Office had sparked off the scramble into cable, announced that, owing to the lack of progress, it would undertake another study; Mr Maxwell bought Rediffusion's cable business for £9 million. In January 1985 the Cable Authority assumed its full power and by July 1985 it had named the next ten areas for cable licences: Bolton, Camden in north-west London, Cardiff and Penarth, Cheltenham and Gloucester, Edinburgh, central Lancashire (including Preston, Leyland and Chorley), Southampton and Eastleigh, Tower Hamlets and Newham in east London, Wandsworth in south London, and west Surrey. Yet by the early summer of 1985 the sum total of activity with new cable in Britain was as follows.

Aberdeen Cable had started laying its system and opened for business, charging £16.95 a month for a take-it-or-leave-it package of fifteen channels.

Swindon Cable was in operation offering a basic package of four new channels at £5.95 a month plus a movie channel for an extra £8 a month, but only about 12 per cent of houses passed by the cable were subscribing.

Westminster had a few houses hooked up to an experimental system.

Croydon Cable was laying its network.

Clyde Cable Vision had finally raised £30 million capital after a nine-month struggle and planned to open a twenty-channel service in Glasgow in October.

Before it had even begun the rush into cable seemed to have slowed to a crawl. The chief reason, depending upon whom you listened to, was the change in the tax laws, new plans for DBS in Britain, the public's passion for video recorders, or a swift reversal in the fortunes of the cable industry in the US which, after booming for several years and inspiring wild optimism among some of Britain's would-be cable barons, stumbled heavily in 1983–4.

Britain's plans for direct broadcasting by satellite had run into even bigger difficulties. First the BBC decided that the cost was too great for them alone and they formed a consortium in which they held a 50 per cent interest, ITV held 30 per cent, and the other 20 per cent was taken by five independent firms: Consolidated Satellite Broadcasting, Granada TV Rentals, S. Pearson, Thorn EMI, and the Virgin group. With fifteen ITV companies, the five other firms and the BBC this became known as 'the Club of 21'. The British Government, unlike its counterparts on the Continent, refused to make any contribution to the launching of DBS. Yet, as with cable, while the Thatcher administration preached *laissez-faire* on the one hand, on the other hand they attempted to impose government rules. In the case of DBS the rule was to buy British, the hope being that this would sustain the national aerospace industry. However, the Club of 21 insisted that they could only run the system economically if allowed to buy their hardware at the lowest possible price on the world market. Eventually, in June 1985, the Club of 21 plan was dropped. It was too risky, said the participants, and the ten-year franchises suggested by the Government were too short. Even the Government's additional offer to extend the ITV companies' existing terrestrial licences as a quid pro quo for risking the move into the celestial sphere failed, in the end, to tempt them. They felt more sure of passing muster at the licensing review on the ground in 1989 than of making a profit in the skies on DBS within ten years. In July 1985, as soon as that scheme had been abandoned, there was talk of an ITV 'Super Channel' beaming Britain's most popular commercial programmes by low-power satellite (not DBS) to European cable systems. The plan was outlined to a meeting of the International Advertising Association by Brian Tesler, managing director of London Weekend Television and chairman of ITV's Cable and Satellite Working Party (which had done so much work on the Club of 21 DBS scheme). His description made no secret of the huge advantage to exporters in producing English-language programmes – thanks largely to the Americans, of course – and the eagerness of Europeans to take British rather than American programmes in English.

In 1979 Harold Wilson had warned that in the 1980s Britain would be 'invaded' by European television programmes beamed down upon us from satellites. Tesler's address made it clear that in the immediate future, with 50 per cent of socio-economic class AB residents in

Europe speaking fluent English, the prospects were precisely the opposite. The Super Channel, he said,

> will deliver a targeted, segmented and up-scale audience to trans-national advertisers by aiming its programme output at definable targets at different times of day: business people during breakfast with TV-am; women during the morning with leisure programmes and in the early evening with soap operas and game shows; children during the afternoon with cartoons, drama and magazines; family audiences in the heart of the evening with popular entertainment ranging from *Coronation Street* to *The Professionals*, from *Winner Takes All* to *Benny Hill*; sports fans in the later evening; and young people throughout Europe late at night with distinctive programming ranging from *The Tube* to *Spitting Image*.

The hunger of European audiences for this sort of popular British programming had been established by the eagerness with which Continental viewers took to Rupert Murdoch's Sky Channel and picked up (legally or illegally) British television transmissions all along the North Sea coast. The BBC quickly made clear their own possible interest in joining the Super Channel, their concern, like ITV's, being to establish an early presence in the satellite business and ensure that the new freebooters – Rupert Murdoch, Robert Maxwell, Ted Turner and so on – did not monopolize the new technology. While all this talk went on, DBS schemes in France, Germany and Japan were going ahead.

In Britain, with DBS delayed indefinitely, the national cable revolution postponed, and leading home computer firms finding the boom transformed to a slump, it seemed as though the age of information was temporarily receding instead of approaching. Yet there is little doubt that, in an industry so utterly dependent upon complicated modern technology, change certainly will occur. Whether the agent of change will be cable, low power satellites, DBS or all three – or some other as yet undeveloped technology – is impossible to say. One thing does seem clear, however. The new technologies are not going to be introduced into a vacuum; we are not, so far anyway, talking about technologies which will bring with them new mass media in the way that the film camera brought cinema and the wireless system brought radio. These new technologies will arrive as additions to or modifications of an existing mass medium and one which has already been colonized by mighty imperial powers.

In Britain the two most important are clearly the BBC and ITV and it is impossible even to begin to make sense of the likely future of British television without first considering their structure and background. Even supposing for a moment that either organization or both were to disappear owing to the arrival of new technologies – a highly unlikely prospect – their shaping of the first fifty years of British television would still be immensely influential both on the newcomers and on the whole future of television.

CHAPTER FOUR

Ally Pally and the Synchronized Experience

There are many major differences between the BBC and ITV. They began differently, their constitutions are different, their structures are different, their finances are different, their organizations work in different ways, there are even differences between the sorts of people who make up the two systems. And yet to a foreigner it would not be the differences that were so striking but the similarities, especially where it counts most: in the programmes on screen. Tell Americans that *Upstairs Downstairs* and *The Jewel in the Crown* were made not by the BBC but by commercial television, and ninety-nine out of a hundred will not believe you.

The BBC started out not as a high-minded body of public servants but as a collection of wireless manufacturers who banded together in 1922 to form the British Broadcasting Company (not Corporation), of which Lord Riddell said succinctly: 'The people who are at the back of it are not philanthropists, they are businessmen.' No doubt he was right and they did intend that the BBC's programmes should encourage the sale of their wireless sets.

Yet there is no denying that John Reith, the Company's first general manager, believed passionately in the public service ideal and, according to historian Asa Briggs in *The Birth of Broadcasting* (Oxford University Press, 1961), during the last months of the British Broadcasting Company's existence 'its directors connived at their own extinction and did not seek to interfere with the constitutional rearrangements which transformed the BBC from a Company to a Corporation on 1 January 1927'. It actually became a public corporation set up by Royal Charter, operating under a licence and agreement granted by the Home Secretary. Having explained this the opening paragraph of the BBC constitution says pithily: 'The Corporation's object is to provide a public service of broadcasting for general reception at home and abroad.'

In order to do that today, the BBC runs 2 national television networks, 4 national radio networks, and 32 local radio stations in Britain. Its external services broadcast to 100 countries in 37 languages. It employs nearly 30,000 staff and is the country's greatest patron of the arts by a wide margin, supporting 6 orchestras and spending more than the Arts Council on the arts every year. BBC Radio alone commissions more than 300 original plays annually and in 1983 offered 15,000 engagements to actors. In a year the BBC transmits 14,000 hours of television and 170,000 hours of radio. Alasdair Milne, Director-General, boasts that the BBC is the biggest programme-maker in the world and believes that as such the Corporation can survive and even flourish in the age of new technology, provided it is not destroyed by political forces, because: 'What do all the new technologies need? Programmes. And there are very few good programme-makers in the world.'

The external services are financed by a grant-in-aid from the Government amounting to £80 million in 1984–5, but the BBC's domestic broadcasting is supported almost entirely by licence fees. BBC Enterprises which sells programmes abroad, and BBC Publications which publishes *Radio Times*, *The Listener* and books, contributed profits of £11.2 million in the year ending March 1984. The licence fee (at that time £46) has to be paid by anyone in Britain wishing to operate a television receiver, even those who claim that they never watch BBC programmes but stick rigidly to ITV, a vociferous band whose dislike of the licence fee is considerably keener than their sense of honesty, judging from audience research which shows, as you might expect, that virtually everybody watches the

BBC from time to time. In 1984 licence fees totalled £758.7 million, of which £56.7 million was deducted for collection costs, leaving £702 million. In all, the BBC spent £721 million on its domestic services for the year, split 7:3 between television and radio, and it was at the end of that year that it asked the Government for a £19 rise in the licence. In 1927 when the BBC first became a corporation the licence fee was 10 shillings (50p) and there were almost 2.3 million licence-holders so that income was just over £1 million. At that date, however, the entire British broadcasting system consisted of one radio network.

But the BBC remained an all-radio outfit for only ten years. In 1936 it launched the world's first high-definition television service from Alexandra Palace on top of a hill on the northern edge of London. It transmitted programmes for two hours a day, six days a week, and in order to see it you had to live in south-east England and pay £100 (which would buy a reasonable motor car in 1936) for a 10 × 8 inch (25 × 20 cm) black and white television set. The first major television outside broadcast was mounted in 1937 for the coronation of King George VI and the audience swelled to 50,000. But on 1 September 1939 without any warning the screens went blank. Two days later war was declared and the screens stayed dark for seven years.

The service returned in 1946, the Wembley Olympics were televised in 1948, and in 1950 Richard Dimbleby, father of David and Jonathan, and the Robin Day of his era, took part in a programme using the first live link between Britain and the Continent, provided by a new under-sea cable. It was called *Calais en Fête* and featured everybody from dancing girls to town councillors. But once again it was a coronation that really pushed television forwards: the crowning of Queen Elizabeth II in 1953 was the first occasion that ever drew the British together to witness an event as an entire nation.

State papers released under the thirty-year-rule in 1983 showed that members of the 1953 Conservative Government opposed the use of television cameras inside Westminster Abbey but the royal family with a far better nose for the public mood than any mere politician persuaded them to change their minds. The cameras went in with Richard Dimbleby as commentator, and on the day anyone in Britain who had a television set invited their less privileged neighbours in to watch. For many people now in middle age that coronation programme was the first they ever saw and the effects were profound. There were more viewers per set on 2 June 1953 than ever before or since and the audience topped 20 million, exceeding that of radio for the first time.

Neither the royal family nor television ever looked back. In the year following the coronation the number of licensed sets rose by 50 per cent, and from that day to this no public event has been complete without the television cameras. Indeed, during the planning of major occasions the interests of the participants are no longer paramount; the needs of the viewing millions have become equally significant if not more so and events from golf tournaments to royal weddings are now organized to suit the requirements of the cameras and thus the population at large. Elections are no exception. So far television has been a remarkably 'democratic' medium.

Yet from 1953 onwards nobody has used television more shrewdly than the royal family, which is more popular and secure today than at any time in the last thousand years. Nor were they the only ones whose reputation was enhanced by the coronation: it seems to have established in the British collective subconscious a feeling that the BBC is the natural channel of communication for national occasions; a feeling which was reinforced by BBC coverage of other major events in the years before commercial television became widely available. Even as late as the wedding of Prince Charles and Lady Diana in July 1981, by which date commercial television's ITN News was regularly outpointing BBC News and (by general consent among television critics and broadcasters) doing a better job, 67 per cent of the nation turned back to the BBC for the wedding. Around the world the event attracted the biggest audience in the history of television: an estimated 750 million viewers in 74 countries.

For some people the sense of sharing which television brought to great State occasions such as the 1953 coronation and even to more mundane events (indeed to programmes as banal as situation comedies if they were popular enough) was one of the greatest rewards of the medium in its early years. Philip Purser of the *Sunday Telegraph*, one of our most perceptive and experienced television critics, has clearly always felt this deeply. Writing of his feelings while watching the first BBC television production of Orwell's *Nineteen Eighty-Four*, screened in 1954 a year after the coronation, he says: 'I was vaguely aware that evening of what I now believe to be the unique virtue of broadcast television. I wasn't alone, or with a couple of others, in that poky back room where they kept the TV. I was plugged into a huge nation-wide audience hanging on to every turn in the story.'

Jonathan Miller, a man whose mastery of television has stretched from the chairmanship of the sixties' arts magazine *Monitor* to production of some of the best television Shakespeare ever made – notably his 1975 version of *King Lear* with Michael Hordern – has expressed the feeling even more mystically. It is, he says, 'the peculiar reward of knowing that one's experience of these items, trivia or otherwise, happens to be synchronized with that of innumerable and anonymous others'.

For those of us who have never had an inkling of this seemingly semi-religious sensation of 'synchronized experience' its disappearance will obviously be of little significance. However, those who do sense it, and there may well be millions, will presumably miss it once the new technologies come into their own. Clearly the experience lost its greatest potency once Britain acquired more than one channel; you could never be certain subsequently that other viewers would have seen what you had seen. Yet with anything up to four broadcast channels experience suggests that actually there will usually be millions watching with you.

Cable and video would put an end to all that. By diversifying the output, fragmenting the audience, and transferring the choice of timing from programme-maker to viewer, the new technologies will reduce the number of 'national family' occasions to those few when we shall, presumably, all turn as ever to the live broadcast: manned space shots, World Cup finals featuring our own team, and doubtless the coronation of Charles III.

In the year following the Queen's crowning, 1954, Britain witnessed the climax of a major campaign calling for the breaking of the BBC monopoly and the introduction of commercial television to Britain. Reith, who by that date had been made a peer, rose in the House of Lords and, with all the considerable Scottish Calvinism at his command, thundered: 'Somebody introduced Christianity into England and somebody introduced smallpox, bubonic plague, and the Black Death. Somebody is trying now to introduce sponsored broadcasting ... Need we be ashamed of moral values, or of intellectual and ethical objectives? It is these that are here and now at stake.'

Far from seeing his likening of commercial broadcasting to smallpox as ludicrously extreme, many people applauded the good lord's righteous wrath. What is more there are people in Britain even today who still see commercial broadcasting in that light, and some who see little to choose between commercial and BBC broadcasting but condemn it all in terms not much less extreme than Reith's. Even more widespread is the view that the new technologies with their likely reliance upon American trivia are today's version of Reith's smallpox, bubonic plague and Black Death.

Reith was not alone in using the word 'sponsored', which was of course meant to make commercial broadcasting sound even more sinister. No doubt he and his allies adopted the term partly as a reaction to the lobbyists who, instead of taking pride in a system which would pay its way, reacted over-sensitively to the traditional British scorn for anything to do with commerce, expunged the word 'commercial' from their every utterance, and referred persistently to 'independent television'. Unfortunately the trick worked, the phrase stuck, and to this day British commercial television is generally known as 'ITV'. Worse, when the lobbying succeeded and the Government set up a body in 1954 to launch and regulate commercial television, it was called the Independent Television Authority, a title which was changed in 1972 but only to Independent Broadcasting Authority when commercial radio was added to its responsibilities

47

thus reversing the order in which events had occurred at the BBC. That was not the only difference.

Structurally ITV differs significantly from the BBC. Though the BBC does have programme production centres in Belfast, Birmingham, Bristol, Cardiff, Edinburgh and Manchester, and outposts in many other places, the great bulk of BBC programmes has always been made in London. From the beginning the BBC tended to be an alliance of engineers, civil servant types and arts graduates, and the Corporation is run as a classic pyramid-shaped British bureaucracy not unlike that to be found in a Royal Navy battleship or the imperial Indian Civil Service.

Programme ideas are suggested by producers to department heads during 'offers' sessions, department heads put together packages and take them to channel controllers, the controllers answer to managing directors (one for television, one for radio), the managing directors report to the Director-General whose functions include that of editor-in-chief, and the Director-General is answerable to the Board of Governors. The Peat Marwick Report of spring 1985, a value for money review of the BBC's domestic services, noted approvingly that the Managing Director of BBC television (Bill Cotton at that time) was contemplating the replacement of the two channel controllers with controllers for different programme areas, a move which would represent the most radical alteration in the management of BBC television for many years. Cotton's plan was to have five controllers responsible respectively for drama, factual programmes, entertainment, sport and outside broadcasts, and news and current affairs. The idea was to reduce duplication of effort, increase management accountability, and avoid fragmentation in programme production. Following the approving noises from Peat Marwick, the plan was due to go forward for the endorsement of the governors in July 1985.

None of this, however, seemed likely to alter the habitual means of decision-making and trouble-shooting within the BBC which is known as 'reference up', a system in which editorial dilemmas are passed up the chain of command until they reach a level at which they can be resolved.

ITV evolved in a different way and, naturally enough, ended up with a completely different structure. In 1954 the Government set up the ITA, appointing to the original Authority eight members selected from the list of The Great And The Good, the same list from which BBC governors are chosen. Sir Kenneth Clark who was later to present the superb BBC arts series *Civilisation* was the Chairman, and the first Director-General was Sir Robert Fraser, an Australian who had been a journalist and, causing some scandal, a Socialist before becoming a civil servant. Members were chosen not for any known expertise in broadcasting, though film critic Dilys Powell was one of the original eight, but in the long-established British tradition of the gifted generalist. So far, so like the BBC, but then the differences start.

CHAPTER FIVE

Barons Bearing Bubonic Plague

The Independent Television Authority did not intend to expand organically as the BBC had done, spreading from a small southern organization into a national broadcasting network. Instead they set out to construct a national federation of regional programme production companies, each with the sole rights to the sale of advertising time in its own area, each making special programmes for its own locality, and each contributing programmes of wider appeal for broadcasting on the national network.

In 1954 the Authority advertised for contractors and received twenty-five applications, most of them from people involved in show business, industry and newspapers; interests which to this day have a powerful influence on the management side of ITV. Among the first applications was one from Granada, the company controlled by the Bernstein family with holdings in theatre, property and cinemas. Cecil Bernstein provided the input from the variety theatre and brother Sidney, then working in cinema but with a deep interest in Labour politics and in current affairs, brought in a group of bright young newspapermen including David Plowright who in 1985 was approaching his tenth anniversary as Managing Director of Granada TV.

Granada is the only member of the 'Big Five' to have been in at the birth of the ITV system and survived to the present day. The Big

Five are the programme production companies which between them make the lion's share of ITV's nationally networked programmes. Today they are Central (whose contract covers the English Midlands), Granada (the north-west of England), London Weekend (Greater London from Friday night to Monday morning), Thames (London for the rest of the week) and Yorkshire. In contrast to the American system of 'rolling' licences which are automatically renewed unless some particular challenge to the company is raised, British licences are granted for specific periods, a fact which causes growing discontent as the ITV companies face an increasingly uncertain and challenging future. The months before one of the periodic reviews are an anxious time for the companies as they compete to produce especially worthy programmes to impress the Authority, yet licences are renewed much more often than not. For instance, the review which granted eight-year contracts starting in January 1982 resulted in the following companies coming through virtually unscathed with renewed contracts: Anglia (serving East Anglia), Border (Scottish Borders, Lake District, Isle of Man), Channel (the Channel Islands), Grampian (the north of Scotland), Granada, HTV (Wales and the west of England), London Weekend, Scottish (central Scotland), Thames, and Ulster (Northern Ireland).

Yorkshire Television and its associated company Tyne Tees (serving the north-east of England) were also given renewed licences with the requirement that they ceased to operate as wholly owned subsidiaries of Trident Television, and the only two companies which actually lost their licences were Southern (serving the south of England) and Westward (serving the south-west of England) which were replaced by TVS and TSW. At the same time the IBA granted a new licence to TV-am not as a regional production company but as a breakfast television company broadcasting nationwide.

Geographical organization is only the first of the major differences between ITV and the BBC; responsibility for programme transmission is also quite different. Whereas the BBC makes its own programmes and broadcasts them on its own transmitters, which it designs and builds itself, the job is split in ITV: the companies make the programmes but the IBA owns the transmitters and does all the actual broadcasting, a job for which it charges the companies about 6 per cent of their income. This being so it is hard to see how Britain's commercial television companies can be considered any more 'independent' than the BBC. It could be argued that they are if anything rather less so, being dependent upon advertisers for revenue and upon the government-appointed IBA for granting them individual contracts and transmitting their programmes. Furthermore the IBA polices the programmes made by the companies, not only ensuring that unworthy items are not transmitted but also ensuring that particularly worthy items are. For instance every ITV regional company is required to include the regular current affairs programmes *World in Action*, *TV Eye* and *Weekend World* in its schedules at specific times. For many years the Authority described such items as 'mandated' programmes and although the phrase has been practically abandoned the rules remain. At the time of writing, the companies are still required to show those current affairs programmes plus ITN's 5.45 and 10.00 p.m. news programmes and the arts programme *The South Bank Show*, and to include specified amounts of religious, educational and local programming in their schedules at particular times. The IBA also ensures that no commercial breaks are inserted in half-hour current affairs programmes, religious programmes, or educational programmes.

The most heavily regulated parts of commercial television, however, are the actual commercials. The companies are not allowed to accept any advertisements connected with religion, charity or politics, a rule under which the *Spectator* was for many years prevented from promoting itself on screen because the IBA judged it to be a political publication while the *Sun*, and indeed every other national newspaper, was allowed to go ahead on the grounds that it was not. Nor is advertising allowed for matrimonial agencies, fortune-tellers, undertakers, betting tipsters, private detectives, or of course cigarettes.

Such limitations have had little noticeable effect upon ITV income which in 1984 amounted to about £930 million, some 96 per cent of which came from advertising. Though limited to six minutes an hour averaged over the day's programmes, commercial breaks can be sold for as much as £80,000 a minute on the national network in peak viewing time. For many years up to the autumn of 1984 the demand from advertisers was greater than the time available and ITV income simply climbed steadily up the graph, rising far faster than inflation. As a result the remark made by Roy Thomson shortly after he was awarded the original contract for Scottish TV, that 'It's just like having a licence to print your own money', has sometimes looked embarrassingly accurate. It was because the companies had been given a unique monopoly in having the sole rights to sell television advertising in their respective areas that the Government introduced a special Exchequer levy which since 1974 has been charged on profits. The companies are allowed 2.8 per cent of their advertising revenue as profits and then taxed 66.7 per cent on the rest. Up to 1984 ITV had contributed £671 million to the public purse via the levy in addition to normal taxes.

Though it does not say so in public the BBC regards the levy system as having one unfortunate effect: there is a clear temptation for ITV companies to plough back into programme-making whatever money would otherwise appear as profits to be creamed off by the Exchequer. That, says the BBC, is one reason why ITV programmes have been looking more and more lush in recent years while BBC programmes have looked less and less glossy. Certainly stories within ITV of extravagant union practices and expensive management habits are legion. Film crews do fly first class, executives do entertain lavishly, technicians do earn enormous sums when overtime stretches into 'double bubble' and then 'golden time', and even Granada, usually ITV's halo-bearer, is famous within the industry for having flown special food out to its staff on location in India for *The Jewel in the Crown*, using money which, it is said, might otherwise have ended up in the Exchequer.

Having made their programmes the ITV companies also behave quite differently from the BBC in arranging their schedule. As a pyramidical bureaucracy the BBC can simply delegate the responsibility for compiling its schedules to its two channel controllers who, with the autocratic power of Renaissance princes (well, perhaps not *quite* that autocratic), can accept, reject or commission programmes from their drama, news, arts and other departments, arranging them in whatever order they choose in consultation with one another and the managing directors and virtually nobody else.

In ITV the parallel process is quite different. Theoretically each of the fifteen companies retains complete autonomy and may show whatever programmes it likes in its own region, provided it complies with the IBA's mandates and requirements on current affairs and so on. In practice most of the national network shows the same programmes most of the time, but the means by which this uniformity is achieved are described even by those who organize it as Byzantine in their complexity.

Simplifying almost to the point of absurdity, what happens is that each of the Big Five contributes programmes to the national schedule in strict proportion to NARAL, Net Advertising Revenue After Levy. In other words, the more profit you make from selling commercials the more programmes you contribute to the schedule, with the result that Thames are the largest programme-providers.

So long as the proportions are worked out with scrupulous care no money ever has to change hands, and in order to reach that desirable position the Programme Controllers' Group (PCG) comprising the programme heads of the Big Five holds a weekly meeting, also attended by a member of the IBA staff, to work out who puts what into the pot and precisely where it will go in the schedule. If the BBC system suggests Renaissance princes, ITV's puts one in mind of medieval barons, depending as it does upon the manipulation of a tangled web of motives: prestige, profit, jealousy, regional pride, revenge, but above all the need to co-operate enough to maintain the system and hold off the common opponent. Over the years the two phrases used most often to convey the atmosphere of these negotiations have been 'smoke-filled rooms' and 'horse trading'.

Special provision is made for contributions from the ten smaller regional companies; whole committees are now dedicated to serving their interests and bringing more of their programmes to the national network. From time to time jealousies flare into skirmishes and one of the Big Five will relegate a series made by one of its colleagues to a late-night slot, causing a tit-for-tat squabble worthy of Tweedledum and Tweedledee. Similarly one of the regional companies will occasionally strike an independent attitude and boast that it can get bigger audiences with its own schedule than with the one thrashed out by the PCG. It happened at TSW in 1984 but it was the independent-minded chief executive Kevin Goldstein-Jackson who rapidly disappeared, not the network schedule.

There is one further difference between the BBC and ITV which is worth mentioning in view of the widespread belief that a legal requirement to 'inform, educate and entertain' forms the very bedrock of British broadcasting. In the winter of 1984 even Stuart Young, Chairman of the BBC, described the trio of functions as 'Charter responsibilities'. Yet the Charter does not appear to specify them as requirements. The preamble to the Charter merely says in the name of the Queen: 'Whereas in view of the widespread interest which is taken by Our Peoples in broadcasting services and of the great value of such services as means of disseminating information, education and entertainment, We believe it to be in the interests of Our Peoples in Our United Kingdom and elsewhere within the Commonwealth that the Corporation should continue to provide broadcasting services ...' That hardly sounds like a stern injunction.

On the other hand the Television Act governing ITV states that the very first duty of the Independent Broadcasting Authority shall be: 'To provide the television broadcasting services as a public service for disseminating information, education and entertainment'. Furthermore the next paragraph requires the IBA to maintain high general standards in content and quality, and a proper balance and wide range in subject matter, to pay proper attention to the times of day when programmes are broadcast and to secure a wide showing for programmes of merit. Other clauses make the Authority responsible for seeing that programmes do not offend against good taste or decency, that they do not incite to crime or lead to disorder or offend public feeling, that sufficient time is given to news, that the news is presented accurately and impartially, that a 'proper' proportion of programmes should be British, and that matters of political or industrial controversy or relating to current public policy are presented with due impartiality.

None of these requirements has ever been imposed upon the BBC. Instead the Chairman of the BBC once gave voluntary assurances to the Government couched in almost precisely the same terms, and from time to time the Governors have renewed those assurances. They are published as an 'annexe' to the BBC licence.

What the licence does say is that the BBC shall broadcast any announcement required by any Government minister at any time, and that the Secretary of State can ban the broadcasting of any programme at any time by giving notice in writing. The BBC is given the right to announce that any such programme or ban has been required by a minister.

Though there was tension and even argument between the Government and the BBC concerning the independence of the Corporation during the 1926 General Strike and the 1956 Suez crisis, there has never in the last thirty years been any serious suggestion that the Government might use these clauses to overrule the intentions of the BBC, not even during the Falklands War when some ministers complained that certain BBC programmes were contrary to the national interest.

It is worth recalling, however, that when Reith recorded his views of the General Strike in his diary reflecting on why Stanley Baldwin and his Government had not taken over the BBC, he wrote: 'They want to be able to say that they did not commandeer us, but they know that they can trust us not to be really impartial.' Perhaps that throws a slightly different light on the fact that no government has ever used its powers over the BBC. Certainly we should not forget that the clauses are still there in the licence, nor accept blithe assurances such as that offered by Lord Windlesham, former Managing Director of ATV, that freedom of the press includes freedom of broadcasting. Says Windlesham in *Broadcasting in a Free Society* (Blackwell, 1980): 'Within the requirements of the law, broadcasters enjoy[ed] the same freedom as print journalists to report and comment on the events, issues and controversies of the day.'

If that were so the IBA would hardly have attracted such scorn ('pusillanimous' and 'craven' were just two of the words used by newspapers to describe their actions) in the spring of 1985 when they suppressed a Channel 4 programme about MI5 tapping the phones of trade unionists and CND leaders. One of the weaknesses of Britain's commercial television system from the public interest point of view is that all the highly placed journalists are in the programme companies; the IBA which is in a position to suppress their programmes is manned by civil servants. In an attempt to justify the Authority's decision to ignore the public interest and toe the establishment line Director-General John Whitney, whose own background is in light entertainment not journalism, said: 'The IBA is a public authority created by statute and is ultimately responsible for the publication of programmes on ITV and Channel 4. *It is subject in its work to legal restrictions and constraints which do not apply to the newspapers and other means of communication.*' [My italics.]

That makes Lord Windlesham's grand claim sound somewhat hollow, and Sir William Rees-Mogg, former editor of *The Times* and at the time of writing Vice-Chairman of the BBC, has made the position even more depressingly clear: 'Newspapers were born free', he says, 'but television was born in chains, a monopoly created by the state, dependent on the state and in every country regulated by the state.' Certainly Britain's broadcasters have never struggled to achieve true independence as Britain's journalists did in the eighteenth and nineteenth centuries. The idea of 'public service' often seems more closely akin to national service than public interest. The pity is that the new technologies, especially DBS which may prove virtually beyond the control of the state for some time at least, could offer true independence for broadcasters and yet be used for little more than light entertainment. It is difficult to imagine any international operator of DBS bothering to investigate MI5's murkier activities.

These then are the fundamental differences between Britain's two broadcasting structures: the BBC is a sixty-year-old organization which started in radio and grew steadily into a monolithic bureaucracy, broadcasting nationally and internationally, financed by a licence fee and characterized by an administration combining civil service habits with senior-common-room tastes, whereas ITV is a thirty-year-old federation of local commercial companies founded by entrepreneurs and supported by advertising, controlled by a government-appointed body which authorizes and transmits its programmes solely within the UK.

CHAPTER SIX

Public Service *v*. Public Taste

The similarities between the BBC and ITV are at least as numerous as, and to most outsiders more remarkable than, the differences. It was no doubt natural that many of the standards and values of Reith's BBC radio service should be extended within the same organization to its television service when that began. Less predictably those same standards and values emerged with considerable strength in commercial television when ITV began. The main reason for this can probably be found in the shared backgrounds and attitudes of BBC and ITV staff at all levels below that of the boards, whether of directors or governors. Even at board level more similarities than distinctions would be noticed by a visiting Martian.

Whatever the original influences and the early staff intake, there are a great many journalists at executive level in both systems today. Indeed large numbers of staff on both sides are BBC-trained journalists because commercial television from the beginning recruited from the Corporation; 'poached' as the BBC would have it. ITV people say this was inevitable since there was no other reservoir of trained personnel (though one company, Granada, recruited a lot of Canadians). The BBC responds grumpily that even today it does most of the training not only for itself but for its competitors too since the relatively small ITV companies have no coherent national training schemes but use their bigger salaries to tempt away every category of BBC staff, from make-up artists to videotape editors, the minute the Corporation has finished teaching them. Thus there is still a flow of influence from BBC to ITV.

The movement is not restricted to technical staff. Paul Fox who was Controller of BBC1 moved to Yorkshire TV and became Managing Director. BBC1's next Controller, Bryan Cowgill, left the Corporation to join Thames TV where he similarly became Managing Director. Melvyn Bragg, not only presenter and editor of *The South Bank Show* but Head of Arts at London Weekend TV, joined the BBC straight from university and worked on *Monitor*, the near-legendary BBC arts magazine with the near-legendary Huw Wheldon, and later on the BBC arts programme *Second House*, before moving to ITV. Paul Bonner spent more than twenty-five years with the BBC and then became Controller of Programmes at Channel 4. And so on.

The movement has not all been one way. Michael Grade who in 1984 was tempted back to Britain from Los Angeles to become Channel Controller of BBC1 and lead the Corporation's drive to recapture bigger audiences used to be Programme Controller at London Weekend TV. His fellow Channel Controller, Graeme McDonald of BBC2, spent years with Granada before joining the BBC. Brian Wenham, Director of Programmes at BBC Television and tipped more often than anyone else as the next Director-General, started his career with ITN. Even the Director-General, Alasdair Milne, the fiercest exponent of BBC values, left the BBC in 1965, worked as a freelance for two years, and joined a consortium to bid for Roy Thomson's Scottish TV contract when it came up for renewal – the one that was like a licence to print your own money.

The shared outlook of BBC and ITV staff is greatly enhanced by the fact that Britain's commercial television system was carefully constructed to keep the 'commercial' separate from the 'television'. In contrast to commercial television in America and many other countries, the British system does not permit sponsored programmes. Furthermore the business of selling advertising time has been separated as much as possible from the business of programme-making, so that the influence of advertisers on programme-makers is minimal or even non-existent. It is true that a half-hour programme on ITV will usually last about twenty-five minutes, and some drama series such as *The Sweeney* tend to be made with three or four 'natural breaks' for commercials in mind. But that aside, Britain's commercial television producers have been distanced and protected as far as possible from the influence of advertisers. It is consequently quite possible for a director or producer to bring precisely the same attitude to bear on a programme whether it is for the BBC or ITV, and those who have worked in both systems will confirm that, apart from occasional technical discrepancies over crewing and better pay in ITV, there is often no noticeable difference between the two.

It would be wrong, however, to imply that the flow of influence between the two systems has been equal in the two directions. Not only is the BBC the older organization with consequently stronger traditions and, thanks to its structure, a coherence which the regional ITV companies lack, but it appears, when compared to even older and bigger organizations, to have an extraordinarily powerful and pervasive ethos. The effect is apparent from the very top to the very bottom of the BBC.

From time to time politicians who have fallen out with the Corporation attempt to saddle the broadcasters with a master who will halt their galloping ambitions, keep them on a tight rein and teach them a little humility. Without exception the attempts fail, the BBC works its magic, and in no time at all the old war-horse is back in the fray spurred on by its new master with all the passion of a recent convert. The most famous instance occurred in 1967 after Harold Wilson, then Prime Minister, began to regard the BBC 'as a conspiracy against him and his government'. The words are those of Lord Hill who was at the time Chairman of the ITA. In what was seen as a deliberate slap in the face for the Corporation, Wilson asked Hill to move straight across from his job in commercial television and take over as Chairman of the BBC following the death of Lord Normanbrook.

Hill did so and received a shocked and cool welcome from his new colleagues who had not even been warned let alone consulted about his appointment. Yet within months Hill was going into the lists face to face against his own champion, Wilson, to persuade him not to take a threatened legal action for libel against the BBC, telling him 'he could sack the Governors but he could not seriously take them to court'. With superb sang-froid Hill writes of this meeting with Wilson in his book *Behind the Screens*: 'Clearly he disliked the BBC. I do not doubt that his belief that the BBC was continuously unfair was genuine. After these exchanges I felt sure that the libel action would be dropped, though he did not say so. He would have to consult his solicitor, Lord Goodman, he said. I then raised the question of increasing the licence fee.' Rather like facing down the Gorgon in her den and then raising the question of funds for the church roof. It seems that the BBC mandarins had done their stuff, turned the new man, and gained another doughty convert.

Suspicion of the BBC's activities and supposed corporate attitudes has not been confined to Labour governments. Any administration which lasts will eventually take against broadcasters because journalists will always tend to pay most attention to those in power. It is far more important, after all, that the electronic branch of the fourth estate should investigate the deeds and misdeeds of the Government than those of the Opposition; hence the tendency for successive administrations to fall out with the BBC whatever their political leanings.

Lord Hill remained Chairman until 1972. He was succeeded by the academic Michael Swann who stayed until 1980 when George Howard of Castle Howard took over. Illness obliged Howard to step down in 1983 and Stuart Young replaced him. Once again doubts were raised about the appointment. Just as in Harold Wilson's time, there had been the mother and father of a row between the Government and the BBC some months previously, this time over a *Panorama* programme which provided a platform for those who opposed the Falklands War. Alasdair Milne, who had gone to the House of Commons to face the Tory back-benchers' Media Committee, told me: 'The first time I spoke they barked "Can't hear you" so I said I'd speak up. Then they shouted "Still can't hear you, stand up." It was like being in Star Chamber. When they got really angry they started waving their order papers and growling like dogs.' It was no secret that the anger with the BBC expressed in those growls was shared by the Falklands victor, Margaret Thatcher.

When the time came shortly afterwards for her to be consulted about a new BBC chairman, and her preference for Young was declared, much interest was caused by the fact that he was a known Conservative sympathizer from Mrs Thatcher's own Parliamentary constituency of Finchley. It was also noted that he had been a BBC governor for less than two years and that David Young, his brother and close friend, had been brought into the Cabinet by Mrs Thatcher. In 1984, the year that Stuart Young became BBC Chairman, his brother received a peerage.

Stuart Young, one of the senior partners in accountants Hacker Young and a director of British Caledonian and Tesco, was known to agree with the Thatcher market philosophy. More, he had even been heard to utter the ultimate BBC blasphemy and suggest that perhaps selling a little bit of advertising time might do the Corporation no harm. His appointment was widely seen as another attempt from Downing Street to inflict the firm smack of government on a wayward BBC.

Yet by the time I interviewed him the following year the mandarins had done their stuff again. He had not merely done a U-turn, recognized the great strength of the uncontaminated licence fee, and taken against the idea of advertising on the BBC, he actually declared that if the Corporation were forced to take commercials, that would be 'anathema' and he would not be able to stay. 'Not even a *little* bit of advertising?' I asked. 'You can't be a little bit pregnant,' he replied. The line had been coined years earlier by Bill Cotton, one of the chief mandarins.

This astonishing ability to take in would-be reformers or rebels and rapidly transform them into chanters of the Corporation creed is almost as effective at the base of the pyramid as it is at the top. Ever since the early sixties when television started to be seen as a glamour industry the BBC has been attracting thousands of job applications. Over the years many who started as 'General Trainees' with privileged entry to the more desirable programme departments have progressed into some of the top positions in British broadcasting. Alasdair Milne was a General Trainee, Melvyn Bragg was another, Alan Yentob was a third. For years now the half-dozen or so annual openings for General Trainees have been oversubscribed not by scores or hundreds of applications but by thousands, many of the applicants being not just holders of university degrees but Oxford and Cambridge graduates with first-class honours.

The Corporation can take its pick of the brightest and the best and at that level of ability they find some fairly independent spirits. But again and again the brainy and bolshie young people who arrive with the intention of exploiting and subverting dear old Auntie (a title the BBC gained in the fifties and lost in the seventies) end up explaining with a rueful smile how they have come to appreciate the virtues of the place. It has been called 'repressive tolerance' and the only people capable of withstanding it for long seem to be the creative few who just don't want to be part of any organization but who live by their wits, work on short-term contracts in plays or documentaries or oddball comedies such as *Monty Python* and *Not The Nine O'Clock News*, and never quite fall into the cushioning warmth of the homogenizing BBC jelly. This category of people became increasingly important as the recruitment pool for the independent sector which mushroomed at the start of Channel 4 and is now producing the most cost-effective programming in the business.

It is not only the continuous seepage of staff from the BBC into commercial television which has spread Corporation values across the full breadth of the British industry. There was always a desire among many ITV people, especially those within the IBA, to be seen as equal to the BBC in terms of public service. The Television Act makes the public service ideal a formal requirement and the IBA's mandating of current affairs, arts, religious and educational programmes is clearly a way of sustaining public service content within a commercial system.

Not that all the ITV companies necessarily need to be dragooned into public service undertakings. Though most were certainly launched with the idea of making money and providing entertainment, when Granada came on the air in May 1956 its opening item was a tribute to the BBC. In the ensuing thirty years Granada – though only one ITV company out of fifteen – has done more than the entire BBC to extend the boundaries of television journalism. Its much imitated current affairs series *World in Action*, its brave determination to bring proper political coverage to television, its documentary dramas developed as a way of communicating events occurring behind the Iron Curtain, its coverage of TUC and Party conferences, its 'hypothetical' series on crisis management and problem solving, and its perpetually inventive coverage of local and general elections, have between them constructed an entire grammar of journalism for the new electronic medium. Since Granada also produced *Brideshead Revisited* and *The Jewel in the Crown*, probably the two best drama serials ever made for television anywhere, there is no doubting that commercial television can equal and even surpass BBC standards of quality.

Moreover, although Granada has proved to be a quite exceptional company in honouring and even inventing its own public service commitments, it is not alone. In 1984 Central TV, which took over the Midlands contract from ATV, launched The Television Trust for the Environment (TVE), a non-profit-making company formed with the United Nations Environment Programme as co-sponsors, to work on the sort of environment subjects in which Central and previously ATV had occasionally specialized. The idea was proposed by Adrian Cowell, the producer responsible for ATV's award-winning documentary *The Tribe that Hides from Man* and Central's *The Decade of Destruction*, both about the crisis in the Amazon jungle. TVE's first undertaking was to send cameraman/director Charles Stewart to East Africa to make a programme about desert erosion. While there Stewart became aware of the Ethiopian famine, broke off from his desert film, and made *Seeds of Despair* which in

July 1984 first caused the crisis to be brought to the attention of the world.

When ITV began thirty years ago, however, the companies' chief concern was not to match the public service ideals of the BBC but to attract a big enough audience to make their new commercial system pay. In the very early months they often adopted BBC ideas – orchestral concerts, Shakespeare, serious documentaries – only to learn from the ratings that it had taken the audience no time at all to discover the art of channel-hopping. At the end of 1956 Roland Gillette of Associated Rediffusion (the company which was later to metamorphose into Thames but which at that time ran the London weekday contract) said: 'Let's face it once and for all, the public likes girls, wrestling, bright musicals, quiz shows, and real-life drama. We gave them the Hallé Orchestra, *Foreign Press Club*, floodlit football and visits to the local fire station. Well we've learned. From now on what the public wants it's going to get.' (Quoted by Peter Black in *The Mirror in the Corner*, Hutchinson, 1972.)

And for a few years that is precisely what happened. By the end of 1957 ITV viewers were being offered action series such as *The Buccaneers* and *The Adventures of Robin Hood*, crime series such as *Shadow Squad* and *Mark Saber*, soap operas such as *Emergency Ward 10*, American series such as *Dragnet*, *I Love Lucy*, *Highway Patrol*, and *Gun Law*, comedies such as *The Army Game* and *The Arthur Haynes Show*, and panel games such as *Yakity-Yak* and *I've Got a Secret*.

Above all ITV offered prize game shows. In 1957 they put out eight of these a week, most of them copied from American originals. They included *Criss Cross Quiz*, *Bury Your Hatchet*, *People Are Funny*, and *Beat the Clock* (later to become the centrepiece of *Sunday Night at the London Palladium*). The two most famous were *Double Your Money* with Hughie Green and *Take Your Pick* with Michael Miles (not to mention Alec Dane on the gong for the 'Yes/No Interlude').

The result was rapid, dramatic, and never to be forgotten by the BBC. In September 1957 Sir Kenneth Clark claimed that the audience was splitting 79:21 in favour of ITV. It was not quite as bad as that every week, but in December 1957 figures from TAM (Television Audience Measurement) showed that in London, out of 539 programmes listed in the Top 10 since ITV began, 536 were ITV and 3 BBC. In the Midlands the BBC scored 2 out of 556 and in the North 2 out of 544. At the Corporation, which up to this point had been the only show in town, it was time for home truths.

In the national debate preceding the arrival of commercial television the belief had of course been expressed that 'No one ever went broke underestimating public taste.' The fear was that by pitching its appeal down market, way below the aim of the Reithian BBC where the idea had always been to raise public expectations a bit by perpetually aiming slightly above the heads of the listeners and viewers, ITV would seduce the bulk of the audience.

Reith's 'bubonic plague' speech with its overtones of contagion suggests that he may well have shared this fear. Yet in the months immediately before the opening of ITV many BBC people had come to believe that quality would out, experience would count, and the British would remain loyal to the Corporation which had seen them through the Second World War with Churchill speeches, honest news reporting and ITMA comedies, albeit on steam radio.

Apart from the Luftwaffe the BBC probably had been Britain's most important unifying force from 1939 to 1945. It is hard to imagine what might have happened during such horrors of twentieth-century warfare as the London Blitz had there not also been twentieth-century communication systems such as BBC Radio. But by the mid fifties the war was the very last thing the British wanted to hear about, and when it came to switching on the television after a hard day's work very few people seemed to think about loyalty to some distant plum-in-the-mouth Corporation. They thought about entertainment.

Peter Black, who was at that time, and for many years afterwards, television critic of the *Daily Mail*, wrote an excellent book about the coming of commercial television to Britain, *The Mirror in the Corner* (Hutchinson, 1972), in which he remarked: 'The audience's good will towards the monopoly [i.e. the BBC] turned out to be an illusion. Once they had a choice the working-class audience left the BBC at a pace that suggested ill will was more deeply entrenched than good ... That most of the audience sincerely disliked Shakespeare, good music, serious documentaries – art of any but the simplest and most familiar kind – and would turn them off at once if another TV service was offering a light alternative, had been prophesied and indignantly denied all through the debates. Its truth was now demonstrated with piercing force.'

The speed with which the public deserted the BBC was of course both shocking and alarming for those at the Corporation. The question to be answered today, however, is whether we really believe that it would have been better to keep commercial television out of Britain, allow the BBC to go on running its monopoly service with its worthy drama, its hypnotically repetitive 'interlude films' showing a potter's wheel or an aquarium of fish in the gaps between programmes, and its well-intended general knowledge quizzes (*Animal Vegetable Mineral* manned by archaeologists and academics was regarded as almost frivolous), and simply put up with the Corporation's failure to satisfy the desire of most viewers – proved conclusively by the arrival of ITV – for much lighter entertainment, hoping that one day the BBC might have seen the light all by itself.

The effect of ITV's successful raid on the audience was indeed to 'lower' the median level of British broadcasting. In order to win the audience back the BBC had to learn how to modify some of its existing programmes and, more significantly, try to make programmes which could compete successfully against soap operas, game shows, and schmaltzy variety. For the first time in the history of British broadcasting, ratings had become very important.

In the event the BBC did change its ways; much of its output did become more popular; it did start to claw back ratings. The Corporation, having had such a powerful influence on the attitudes and early ideals of ITV, found that the tables had been turned. Now the BBC was obliged to start learning how to meet the demotic appeal of commercial television by developing its own brand of populism. The social and constitutional similarities mentioned earlier began to have their counterpart in similarities on screen.

It all sounds ominously like the perfect paradigm for those who argue that with the new television technologies of the eighties more will mean not diversity but more of the same, a narrowing instead of a broadening of choice, and a vertical dive towards the lowest common denominator as an increasing number of competitors fight for the biggest possible audience share.

Yet the fact is that practically nobody inside the television industry and very few outside would argue today that the coming of ITV had proved to be a disaster. On the contrary, the arrival of the brash newcomer and the shock it sent through the BBC system is seen as precisely the stimulus that was needed to stir up a somewhat stagnant, old-fashioned, and complacent organization and force it to try out a host of fresh ideas. Some of those ideas materialized in programmes which are now regarded as marking the highest pinnacles television has achieved.

That is not to say that in the late eighties we should consequently usher in every crazed cable merchant and satellite operator on the grounds that they will automatically do for today's cosy BBC/ITV duopoly what ITV did for the sleepy BBC monopoly of 1955. But it is to say that when we hear people likening the encroachment of the new technologies to the coming of the plague, the new brand of would-be broadcasters condemned as the greedy men of commerce, and the warning that this new lot will value none of the gentlemanly ideals which are shared with such passionate conviction by BBC and ITV, we should stop a moment and try to remember why it all sounds so familiar.

CHAPTER SEVEN

The Six-Five Special (Just in Time)

Although they had lost viewers the people at the BBC did not lose their heads. It was clear that quite a lot of ITV's audience consisted of those who had just acquired their first television sets. As the smaller ITV stations opened region by region, with Channel TV completing the network in September 1962, so television sales and rentals increased. In 1955 5 million British homes had televisions; by 1958 the figure had doubled. One of the side-effects was a rapid increase in the BBC's income from licence fees, but that was no great consolation when it was clear from the TAM ratings that ITV was taking the lion's share of the new viewers.

The BBC began to formulate series aimed at a wider socio-economic spectrum than hitherto; in other words it started making programmes for people who were poorer, younger, and not as well educated as the BBC's traditional middle-class viewers. Starting with the area where it was traditionally strongest, news and current affairs, the BBC launched *Tonight* from Grace Wyndham Goldie's department early in 1957 to help fill the period which had previously been known as 'The Toddlers' Truce'. This was the hour between 6.00 and 7.00 p.m. when transmission had closed down so that mothers could hustle their children off to bed without any temptation for them to stay up and watch 'just five minutes more'. Cliff Michelmore was *Tonight*'s chatty and beaming anchorman, and many of the staff were recruited from the ruins of the only good photographic news magazine Britain had ever had, *Picture Post*. The *Post* had concerned itself very much with the lives of ordinary people, and when *Tonight* took on the gangling Scottish reporter Fyfe Robertson, Macdonald Hastings (father of Max), the urbane Kenneth Allsop, bespectacled Trevor Philpott and Slim Hewitt, his photographer who became a cameraman, all from the *Post*, the new programme became a comparable voice of the people. As such, it was in sharp contrast to the traditional BBC current affairs programmes such as *Panorama*, presented by Richard Dimbleby, which tended to be widely regarded as the voice of the Establishment.

No doubt some would argue that the coming of ITV had thus had the effect of lowering the tone of BBC journalism. After all, where *Panorama* was grave and studied and given to lengthy consideration of a few weighty topics, *Tonight* was irreverent (by the prevailing standards), fast, sharp, modern, inquisitive, given to skipping from item to item, and presented live in a manner which sometimes hinted at barely ordered chaos only just off-camera – sometimes not even off. In the studio Cy Grant sang topical calypsos, and outside the reporters specialized in getting themselves into the thick of things, whether it was a question of danger or fun.

Was this an example of the competitive drive for ratings leading to a lower common denominator? For the BBC *Tonight* certainly did the trick: opening in February with an audience of 1 million it climbed to 5 million by the end of the year. But if today we wish to sustain the argument that *Tonight* was an illustration of more meaning worse, of competition driving down standards, then we have to smash our way through a thicket of praise and adulation not to mention dewy-eyed nostalgia which has grown up around the programme since it closed in 1965.

To fill the 6.00–7.00 slot on Saturday nights when *Tonight* was off the air the Corporation launched a series which was even less typical of itself. Bill Haley and his Comets had caused riots in 1956 when the film *Rock around the Clock* was released in Britain and in December of that year Associated Rediffusion had launched the pop music series *Cool for Cats*. The BBC responded on Saturday evenings from February 1957 with *Six-Five Special* presented by Pete Murray and Josephine Douglas who introduced new young singing stars and their hits. The signature tune went

> It's the Six-Five Special comin' down the line
> It's the Six-Five Special right on time

and it could be argued that in that banal and misrhyming couplet the whole history of the decorous British Broadcasting Corporation was being disastrously rewritten. Then again you could argue that a modern means of communication which was nothing if not a *mass* medium was finally beginning to come into its own.

The truth was that although still operating on just one channel the BBC was maintaining its traditional middle-class Reithian output – *World Theatre*, *Panorama*, *Concert Hour*, *The Brains Trust* – but at last, after running a television service for more than ten years, it was introducing a bigger proportion of the kind of programmes most viewers wanted. In 1958 the pace increased. The BBC started *The Sid Caesar Show* and *The Black and White Minstrel Show*, a smash-hit song and dance formula which lasted twenty years and was only dropped in 1978 because race had become such a touchy subject.

The same year saw the BBC launch its sports magazine *Grandstand*; the gory documentary series *Your Life in their Hands*, a sort of trepanner's delight dwelling endlessly on the wonders of modern surgery; and *Blue Peter*, which has proved the longest-running children's programme on British television, having passed its twenty-fifth birthday some years ago. *Blue Peter* still has a mixture of male and female presenters who bring their pets with them into the studio, and these days the male presenters tend to do the cooking (which always seems to involve bananas or melted chocolate or crumbled digestives and usually all three) while their female counterparts do the heavy digging in the *BP* garden. But in the dear dead days of 1958 when 'sexism' had not even been invented the first female presenter was Leila Williams – Miss Great Britain 1957.

So the dogged fight back against ITV went on and innovations at the more popular end of the spectrum continued. It was not an isolated occurrence. Bernard Davies, for many years television critic of *Broadcast* magazine, and one of the most astute Britain has had, wrote in No. 886 (1 November 1976):

> There was, growing through the years of Attlee's social democracy and the Fabian trends of post-war politics (a gradual but inevitable movement leftwards) a new kind of society in which the non elite did not know their places and were progressively more and more insistent that the things they did and the ways they did them were just as valid and important as the shibboleths of formal culture. Opposing 'monopoly' was not just a protest about a certain kind of organization but a deeply-rooted movement against 'middle class' and conventional standards of culture.

In newspapers, music, book publishing and elsewhere the same forces were at work, and today we are experiencing another surge of feeling of a similar kind. This time, however, the expectation is not so much of an increase in popular culture but of an increase in personal choice and control. It is in a sense the beginning of Alvin Toffler's 'third wave'. VCRs have introduced viewers to the idea that having broadcasters dictate the timing of programmes is not an unchangeable rule. Thanks to their recording machines viewers who want to take a triple-strength dose of *Crossroads* once a week on Sunday morning can do so, even though the programme is transmitted on three weekday evenings. Viewers clearly welcome the trend away from enslavement to the broadcasters' schedule even if it does mean a reduction in 'synchronized experience'.

In the late fifties the BBC's drive for ratings went on; 1959 saw the launch of *Juke Box Jury*, a pop music quiz chaired by David Jacobs in which the panel had to vote on whether new records would be hits or misses. Next year the Corporation started *Face to Face*, an almost inquisitorial interview series in which the spotlight was literally turned on some public figure who was interrogated, sometimes quite fiercely, by John Freeman. (Later, after he had been ambassador to Washington, he became Chairman of London Weekend TV.)

Face to Face appeared in 1960; the same year that Hugh Carleton

Greene, brother of novelist Graham Greene, became Director-General of the Corporation. The first thing you notice about Hugh Greene is that he is very tall and the first thing a lot of people learn about him is that he is very tough and does not suffer fools gladly. Since he also has more than a touch of that eccentricity which seems to mark so many of the family dynasties from England's upper-middle-class intelligentsia (the Mitfords, the Huxleys, the Longfords) he is a formidable character to put in charge of an organization with as much potential as the BBC.

In *Ah! Mischief: The Writer and Television* (edited by Frank Pike, Faber, 1982), dramatist David Hare tells the story of researching his outstanding television play *Licking Hitler*, finding that one of the people who knew most about wartime broadcasting was Hugh Greene, and going round nervously to explain to Greene that he was planning a play about black propaganda in the Second World War:

> 'There can only', he [Greene] said ominously, 'be one reason why a writer like you could possibly be interested in that subject; to make mischief.' At once he broke into the broadest smile, and rubbed his hands together. I have never seen a man so delighted by a single word. How attractive that spirit is in him, how fine the BBC was when he ran it, how much that sound working principle – 'ah, mischief!' – is needed there today.

Greene's promotion did indeed mark the start of a completely different era in British television. He threw open the doors and windows and let great blasts of fresh air into the circular corridors of the BBC Television Centre. Within a couple of years attitudes and atmospheres were revolutionized. ITV, which had been making all the running and watching Auntie BBC gamely raising her skirt an inch or two to keep up with the slick young commercial challenger, suddenly found a transformed Corporation not following fashion but setting it.

In the year 1962 alone the BBC launched the satire wave by spinning off *That Was The Week That Was* (*TW3*) from the *Tonight* programme at weekends. It opened a new school of tough, realistic, and popular drama with the Merseyside police series *Z-Cars* which was copied endlessly and which itself spun off *Softly Softly* and

Barlow. It presented the wildly popular series *Dr Finlay's Casebook* – first of a long line of respectable middle-class drama serials – and the arts series *Monitor* showcased Ken Russell's superb biographical film *Elgar*.

Most notable of all, perhaps, in 1962 the BBC started *Steptoe and Son*, the first of a new generation of half-hour comedies which consisted neither of comedians telling gags nor of nuclear families delivering silly one-liners. Instead writers Galton and Simpson, who had just parted company with Tony Hancock, offered pathos, acute social observation and a peculiarly poignant view of modern mores as seen via the life of a whining old rag-and-bone man and his absurdly ambitious grown-up son (Wilfrid Brambell and Harry H. Corbett). The series made history in several ways: it attracted audiences as big as 22 million and was the first of a string of British successes to cross the Atlantic under 'format deals' and take America by storm. In the US the junk dealers became black and the title was *Sanford and Son*. But the particular importance of *Steptoe* here is that the series vividly illustrates all the trends occurring within British broadcasting at the time: the BBC was suddenly the market leader and this was one of the BBC series which brought that about; Reith's middle-class values were being diluted and here was a series set in a junkyard, the most stereotypically working-class milieu imaginable; audiences were being wooed back from ITV and *Steptoe* was one of those that won astounding ratings. Would the Corporation ever have made it without the stimulus provided by the opening of ITV? No one can say for sure, but it seems unlikely.

The suddenness with which the BBC switched from being a follower of ITV where popular programmes were concerned to being the arbiter of television fashion should have been quite startling but at the time was obscured by other social upheavals. At home there was Beatle-mania, the Profumo scandal, Sunday colour supplements, 'the death of God' (marked by the book *Honest to God*), mass civil disobedience by the Committee of 100, and the Great Train Robbery. Abroad there was the Cuban missile crisis, American race riots, war between China and India, the death of Pope John XXIII and then the assassination of President Kennedy. It was a bizarre period when shock was piled upon shock so that at the time the astounding transformation of the BBC appeared comparatively unsurprising.

Looking back now, however, it seems clear that it was at about this time that the BBC with, at first, only a little help from ITV, brought about two closely connected major changes. First they improved the standards of television drama and comedy out of all recognition; and secondly they made it fashionable, with their new approach to current affairs and satire, for television to be watched not only by the middle-class and middle-aged who made up the bulk of the BBC's traditional constituency, and the 'never had it so good' working class who made up the bulk of ITV's, but also by the intelligentsia and those who, thirty years previously, had been called Bright Young Things. *TW3* was watched in Oxford senior common rooms, and Hampstead dinner parties would decamp *en masse* from the dining-table to watch it wherever the set was kept.

With Greene at the top of the BBC determinedly keeping the fuming members of various 'clean-up TV' campaigns at arm's length, the Corporation's young turks started building enthusiastically on the new foundations. Among the mass-audience pullers they launched in 1964 was *Top of the Pops*. Among the high-quality series was *The Wednesday Play*. It is this sequence of single dramas which stands above all as a monument to the quality, the excitement and the inventiveness of that era. Today it is fashionable to pooh-pooh the notion of a golden age of television in the mid sixties, but looking down the list of credits for *The Wednesday Play* merely for its first twelve months it is difficult to avoid the feeling that it *was* a golden age.

James MacTaggart was the most important producer; directors included Philip Saville, Christopher Morahan, Ken Loach, Don Taylor, and Brian Parker, all of them now with international reputations; and the list of writers looks like an awards ceremony: John Hopkins, Hugh Whitemore, Dennis Potter, David Mercer, Troy Kennedy Martin and a dozen more. That opening year ended with MacTaggart producing and Loach directing Nell Dunn's *Up the*

Junction, a raw and bawdy account of working-class life in Battersea which may look dated and a little self-conscious today but was a revelation in 1965.

Some have argued that since the man responsible for the BBC Drama Department at the time was Sydney Newman who had been developing his ideas for *Armchair Theatre* at ITV, it was really ITV which began the sixties drama revolution. There is some truth in this; it would be wrong to imply that all the sixties innovation came from the BBC, and with *Armchair Theatre* ITV did help lead the way into the new era. But the significant point is that Newman made his move in 1963 from ITV to the BBC. He has always been a man with an acute sense of where the vanguard is and which way it is heading. It is typical of him that having returned to his native Canada for some years in the seventies and eighties, he came back to London in 1984 to make drama for Channel 4 with one of the new independent companies: to be up at the frontier again, effing and blinding in the same amiable way and resolutely shoving out the boundaries.

In the year after *Up the Junction* the BBC's offerings included *The Frost Report* which featured Ronnie Corbett and Ronnie Barker working together, plus John Cleese, Graham Chapman, Michael Palin, Terry Jones and Eric Idle – in other words the entire *Monty Python* crew. The Corporation also produced *Cathy Come Home*, the story of the break-up of a young family and probably the most famous single drama ever screened on British television (it led to the foundation of the campaign for the homeless, Shelter) and launched upon an amazed world Johnny Speight's monstrous cockney right-winger Alf Garnett in *Till Death Us Do Part*.

The Corporation was not ignoring the mass audience: in addition to *Till Death* 1966 saw the first of the staggeringly popular inter-national knockabout games series *It's a Knockout*, and the pop shows and variety carried on. But the real triumph of British television in the sixties was that it found ways of making programmes which achieved respectable ratings – *Cathy Come Home* was watched by almost 10 million, the sort of figure that is expected for *Top of the*

Pops or *News at Ten* – and at the same time won critical acceptance and immense prestige.

In the second half of the sixties the British television system settled into a pattern which might be described as benevolent asymmetry. Between the opening of BBC2 on 20 April 1964 and the opening of Channel 4 on 2 November 1982 the Corporation ran two channels against ITV's one. Occasionally this asymmetrical arrangement was described by the more voracious representatives of ITV as 'unfair' but for most of the time it seemed to keep most broadcasters remarkably happy. The BBC with its two channels regularly attracted about 50 per cent of the audience thus maintaining its claim on the licence fee, and ITV with its single channel took the other 50 per cent and easily sold all its advertising time.

Innovation did not cease. The BBC launched *The Forsyte Saga* in 1967, first of a chain of classic serial adaptations which continues to this day. On its first transmission on BBC2 it attracted disappointing audiences but word-of-mouth boosted the repeat on BBC1 to triumphant levels. In 1969 came the anarchic and near-hysterical *Monty Python's Flying Circus*, and also *Pot Black*, a series introduced largely to capitalize on the coming of colour television but which, in the following ten years, led the way to one of the BBC's most dependable ratings winners. ITV launched *News at Ten*, Britain's first regular half-hour news, and *Callan*, the forerunner of many tough special agent series.

So the first fifteen years after the BBC found itself with a competitor proved tremendously fertile. Some series could be said to have 'lowered' standards when measured against those that prevailed during the BBC monopoly but with hindsight a spot of lowering, or more accurately perhaps broadening, seems pretty much what was called for. In attempting to see what lessons from the late fifties and the sixties to apply to the late eighties and the nineties we have to try to decide whether the opening up now of television to an increasingly large number of competitors would mean a further lowering of standards; whether such lowering would be proportional to the number of newcomers or progressive; whether, assuming that standards did change, that might once again be seen one day with hindsight as not such a bad thing; or whether the changes facing us now are of a magnitude so much greater than those described in this chapter that such comparisons are irrelevant.

Is there really something unique about having just two major programme organizations, 'the duopoly', competing for the British viewer rather than three, or ten, or thirty? Many of those who work in the BBC and ITV argue that there is.

CHAPTER EIGHT

The Duopoly and Peaceful Coexistence

Certainly Britain's two television systems did manage to exist and prosper on a remarkably high plateau of achievement throughout the seventies, and in programme terms it seemed that the competition between them was almost entirely beneficial. The pendulum had started with the BBC when the Corporation was providing Britain's only television channel, swung over to ITV in the fifties when the new commercial service lured away the audience, and then back again to the BBC in the golden age of the sixties under Hugh Greene (who remained Director-General until 1969). Now it oscillated rapidly between the two.

The BBC had learned a lesson from ITV and developed its own way of building and pleasing big audiences, but the Corporation had also managed throughout to retain its reputation as the provider of true quality. ITV's image on the other hand still tended to be tainted with that characteristic British disdain for anything commercial which had led to the 'Independent' tag in the first place. There was, by all accounts, no organized campaign by ITV during the seventies to turn the tables once again and start building a reputation for high quality to equal that of the BBC, yet that is what happened and with such success that by the early eighties a dispassionate onlooker might well have judged ITV to have taken over as Britain's standard-bearer for quality television. Thus if the fifties battle was for ratings the seventies battle was for kudos.

In 1969 the BBC began the first of those huge series on the arts and humanities which were to characterize its output in the ensuing decade: *Civilisation*, 13 supremely civilized one-hour talks by Kenneth Clark about the arts from the seventh to the nineteenth centuries, filmed on world-wide locations and unmistakably Reithian in their approach. The series was a sensation both in Britain and the US where PBS showed it over and over again. Three years later came Alistair Cooke's 13-part series *America* about the history and development of the United States; and two years after that Jacob Bronowski's 13-hour series *The Ascent of Man*, which did for the history of science and ideas what *Civilisation* had done for the arts.

In 1973, between the BBC's *America* and *The Ascent of Man*, ITV launched *The World at War*, a colossal undertaking in the overall charge of Jeremy Isaacs at Thames Television. Isaacs later went on to start Channel 4 of which he became the Chief Executive. *The World at War* showed the history of World War II in 26 one-hour episodes, using scrupulously researched archive film from sources all over the world and dozens of new interviews with key personalities. It cost £1 million to make, and like the BBC's blockbuster documentary series it won shelves full of awards in Britain and in the US where Isaacs took an Emmy for 'outstanding documentary achievement'.

In drama too ITV began to subject the BBC to the sincerest form of flattery. With the huge success of the Corporation's *Forsyte Saga* still echoing round the world (in 1970 Russia became the forty-fifth country to buy it), actresses Eileen Atkins and Jean Marsh came up with the idea of a costume drama set in the same period which would look not merely at upper-middle-class members of an Edwardian family but also at the lives of their servants behind the green baize door at 165 Eaton Place. *Upstairs Downstairs* was another monster success on both sides of the Atlantic. The BBC returned the compliment and continued the me-too habit in 1976 by hiring *Upstairs Downstairs* producer John Hawkesworth to make a remarkably similar series, *The Duchess of Duke Street*, for the Corporation.

And so the pendulum swung: after period drama ITV launched into brave and even revolutionary contemporary themes with *The*

Naked Civil Servant, an uncompromisingly honest account of the flamboyant life of homosexual Quentin Crisp; *The Sweeney*, the first British crime series ever to achieve the pace, production standards and sheer exhilaration of America's best action films; and then *Rock Follies*, a uniquely successful episodic television musical with a hilariously outrageous script by Howard Schuman. The BBC responded with Frederick Raphael's brittle but brilliant serial about the graduate over-achievers of the sixties, *The Glittering Prizes*; in the same year a quite unexpectedly popular adaptation of Robert Graves's saga of Roman intrigue, *I, Claudius*; and then Dennis Potter's fascinatingly original *Pennies from Heaven* which played romantic popular songs of the thirties against the grain of a dark and even morbid story about a troubled sheet-music salesman.

Dozens of other good and even great productions poured out of British television during the seventies. Comedies such as *Porridge*, *Fawlty Towers* and *Not The Nine O'Clock News* from the BBC. Factual series such as *Disappearing World*, *The State of the Nation* and *Weekend World* from ITV. The BBC made its drama documentary series *The Voyage of Charles Darwin*, one of the best television series of any description ever made anywhere, in the same year that ITV launched John Mortimer's delightfully entertaining comedy legal series *Rumpole of the Bailey*. Also in the same year (1978) ITV gave us *Edward and Mrs Simpson* and started *The South Bank Show* which rapidly set the standard against which all other arts series had to measure themselves.

It is necessary to give the list in some detail to make the point that this was not a chance flash in the pan; it was not a brief period during which a few good series from the BBC just happened to coincide with a few from ITV. It went on for years and has been continuing in the eighties. In what other country in the world would it be possible for one broadcasting organization in a single year to make five drama serials as good as *The History Man*, *The Hitch-Hiker's Guide to the Galaxy*, *Bread or Blood*, *Private Schultz* and *Maybury*, only to find them all completely overshadowed because in the same year their opponents produced *Brideshead Revisited*? It happened to the BBC in 1981.

As the years pass, 1982 may well be remembered more for the opening of Channel 4 than anything else, but it was also the year that ITV gave us *Muck and Brass*, a fast and powerful serial about corruption in a city centre redevelopment, and the BBC gave us *Boys from the Blackstuff*, an extraordinary drama series in which Alan Bleasdale from Merseyside offered up a *cri de coeur* for all of Britain's unemployed. At such close range it is hard to be sure but there may have been a slight decline since 1982, with only Granada's *The Jewel in the Crown* in 1984 representing an upswing. But then the word 'only' can hardly be applied to *The Jewel in the Crown*. When this tremendous 14-part adaptation of Paul Scott's *Raj Quartet* reached the US, John Leonard of *New York Magazine* said it was 'the best sustained television I've seen in more than thirty years watching' and that was one of the calmer superlatives that were strewn upon it.

Of course, however wonderful *The Jewel in the Crown* may have been, the fact remains that there was much lightweight nonsense and even downright rubbish transmitted on British television during the seventies and eighties. But then it would have been most odd had this not been so, benevolent duopoly notwithstanding. Every mass medium, in fact every medium of expression, is taken up with a lot of mediocre material, plus a little that is good and a tiny proportion that is excellent. The point about British television during the duopoly has been that such an abnormally large proportion of the programmes has been of high quality.

The assertion is not a piece of empty chauvinism even if it does happen to support the claims of those blustering politicians who habitually declare that 'British television is the best in the world' without having any way of knowing whether or not that is true. Thanks to the absurd organization of Britain's Parliament, MPs are the last people to consult about television since they are almost invariably occupied at Westminster in the evening when the public is viewing. The attitude of an awful lot of politicians to television is coloured largely by their own appearances on screen which is what truly concerns them. Consequently on those rare occasions when they hold a formal debate on the subject the ignorance of many would be hilarious were it not so appalling.

Anyone who really is in a position to make international judgements, who has travelled in the last twenty years and watched television abroad, will know that American breakfast television knocks its British counterpart into a cocked hat, that the Swedes are outstanding in contemporary drama, and the Germans excel at televising music. But they will also know that the general level of British television across the entire spectrum has not been matched anywhere. Visitors coming to Britain from abroad frequently say as much and American visitors in particular tend to wax lyrical on the subject.

For those who have watched the decline on a world scale of the British ship-building industry, British football, the Royal Navy, British textiles, and virtually everything else in which Britain once led the world, and who have consequently reached a point where they simply cannot believe that Britain is best at anything, there is furthermore one objective test which has proved again and again that the excellence of British programmes is unmatched. There are today scores of international television 'festivals', and although many of them are really markets largely concerned with programme sales there are a few which are genuinely devoted to the pursuit, recognition and encouragement of excellence. At these festivals British success is unsurpassed.

The oldest of the lot and the one with the greatest prestige, certainly among European broadcasters and probably on a world scale, is the Prix Italia, which started in Capri as a radio festival in 1948. There are several reasons for its high esteem. First the juries do not consist of footballers and fashion models but solely of television producers; the broadcasting organizations which constitute the event send entries for two categories each year and a juror for the third in which they cannot compete. Consequently a producer knows his work is judged by his peers. Secondly it is rare at the Italia to come across the sort of geopolitical carve-up which occurs in so many international juries with Warsaw Pact members ganging up against the rest and vice versa. And thirdly its permanent secretariat and its 'General Assembly' formed by its constituent organizations have always ensured that it does maintain the pursuit of excellence as its chief function.

Radio prizes are still presented, but today more people attend for the television awards. There are three presented annually, one each for drama, documentary and music. In 1984 each was worth 9 million lire (£3,900). There were music entries from Austria, Belgium, Canada, Czechoslovakia, Denmark, France, Germany, Hungary, Ireland, Japan, Norway, Poland, Spain and Switzerland as well as Britain. The winner was the Peter Brook version of *Carmen* initiated by Channel 4 and co-produced with Antenne 2 of France. Twenty dramas were entered and other countries represented in this category included Brazil, Finland, Holland, Italy, Yugoslavia, Korea, Sweden and USA. The winner was ITV with *Made in Britain*, a violent account of skinhead behaviour made by Central TV. The documentary prize went to Japan for *Nuclear Holocaust*.

It would be impressive to take two out of three prizes against world-class competition of this sort just once; no other country has done such a thing in the entire history of the event. Britain has done it not once but several times. Most astonishing of all, in 1978 British broadcasters swept the board, the drama and documentary prizes going to the BBC for *The Spongers* and *Hospital* and the music prize to ITV for *MacMillan's Mayerling*.

A league table of Prix Italia winners between 1957, when television prizes were first introduced, and 1984 looks like this:

Britain 26
France 9
Sweden. 9
Japan 7
W. Germany. 5
Italy 4
USA. 4

Many countries such as Austria, Greece, Hungary, Norway, Russia and Spain have entered regularly but won no prizes at all.

A still more recent international acknowledgement of Britain's television prowess was, if possible, even more emphatic. In the winter of 1984 America's National Academy of Television Arts and Sciences selected 5 programmes out of 144 entries from 25 countries to receive International Emmy Awards. Every single winner was British, though significantly not one came from the BBC: *The Jewel in the Crown* took the drama award for Granada, Channel 4 won the documentary prize with its China series *The Heart of the Dragon* and the music prize with *The Tragedy of Carmen*, and Thames TV won the other two with the comedy *Fresh Fields* and the children's programme *The Wind in the Willows*. It was an achievement quite unprecedented in the history of the Emmy Awards, topped by the presentation of the Directorate Award to Sidney – by now Lord – Bernstein of Granada for 'outstanding contributions over a period of time to the arts and sciences of international television'.

If anything proves that Britain and its peculiar broadcasting duopoly system is a world beater it is surely international recognition such as this.

CHAPTER NINE

De-Regulation and All Out War

Television people might reasonably complain, though interestingly they rarely do, that if any other British undertaking regularly achieved a degree of success on the international stage as great as that of British television it would be the darling of the nation, fêted by politicians, celebrated in the newspapers, and showered with Queen's Awards to Industry. (Contrary to popular belief, conditioned presumably by the quantity of American programmes appearing in peak viewing hours in the UK, Britain earns more from programme exports than she spends on programme imports.) What the broadcasters actually find is that the very system which in their view is responsible for this unique success is now under threat from the Government. As broadcasters in both the BBC and ITV see it, the duopoly has protected them from the need to compete for revenue and left them free to compete in terms of excellence, the result being a world-wide reputation for quality.

Yet so far as they can see, the Government, judging from its willingness to permit a cable invasion and its desire to see DBS introduced, could not care less about preserving the duopoly. To many in the BBC and ITV it appears that the Government is far more interested in possible jobs, new British industries, and exports which might follow upon the de-regulation of television and the coming of the new technologies, than any existing programme excellence. In their view the Government is intent upon ushering into Britain a rabid technological goose which lays tin eggs, albeit lots of them, but which will kill off the existing BBC/ITV goose that has been laying golden eggs for thirty years, largely unnoticed by the politicians whose ignorance of the business is legendary.

Can they not see, cry the BBC and ITV people, that it is only the existence of this odd British hybrid that we call a duopoly which makes such high standards of television possible? Do you not understand that it is by giving the BBC financial security by way of its monopoly on licence fee revenue and giving ITV financial security by way of its monopoly over television advertising that you avoid the awful American system in which everyone has to compete to maximize audiences all the time because they are fighting for the one lot of advertising income? Take away this mutually beneficial British system, they argue, de-regulate television, make everyone including the BBC live by the law of the market-place, and nobody will ever again be able to offer current affairs or serious drama during peak viewing time; they will have to go for the maximum possible audience whether they really want to or not.

If anyone demurs and asserts that the history of broadcasting in Britain is a history of regulation, that the reason British commercial broadcasters show *World in Action* at 8.30 in the evening is because they are told to do so by the IBA, a government-appointed authority, and that there seems no reason why such regulation should not continue, the duopolists reply that regulation can only be enforced so long as income remains secure. 'Take ITV's breakfast television,' they say. 'The IBA's regulations offered a contract for the provision of programmes primarily of news, information and current affairs, and look what TV-am were doing within a year of going on air – Roland Rat, recipes and rock videos, yet the IBA didn't dare even to smack their wrists because it was claimed they were losing so much money and the only alternative was to close down. Do you imagine things will be any different if you allow de-regulation and force ITV to compete with even more Roland Rat?'

This is an argument which not only opposes general de-regulation but any alteration whatsoever to the status quo since it maintains that introducing a little advertising to the BBC would upset the entire ecology of British broadcasting and tear apart the fragile symbiosis of the duopoly. The Corporation line on advertising has always been total resistance from the start on the grounds that if you allow one domino to fall – Radio 1, presumably – the rest will inevitably follow as successive governments decide that it makes more sense to add Radio 2 to Radio 1, and BBC 1 to Radio 2, and so on, than to increase the licence fee. Once the principle is breached, says the Corporation, no government would be able to resist widening the breach rather than increasing taxation. Hence 'You can't get a little bit pregnant.'

There are, however, waiting in the wings ready to step on to the stage with satellites and dishes, cables and star switches, people who not only pour scorn on the cosiness of this BBC/ITV double act ('They would say that wouldn't they, they're very comfy aren't they') but who dissent from the assumptions underlying the duopoly. They are not convinced that British television in its present form is necessarily 'best'. They are not ready to accept that the achievements of the BBC and ITV in the past thirty years – *The Forsyte Saga*, *The Ascent of Man*, *The World at War*, *The Jewel in the Crown*, all the successes and prizes and prestige described in the last chapter – are as important as they have been made to seem.

Of course it is very pleasant, these would-be competitors say, for sophisticated producers to be able to make programmes for an educated élite like themselves who want such things, and nice to be able to export them sometimes too. But let's not forget that television is a *mass* medium. When all those famous British series like *Civilisation* went to the US and caused a 'sensation' were they being shown on the big three commercial networks and scoring high in the ratings and being talked about in shopping malls in Oshkosh and Peoria? Of course not. They were being shown by PBS, America's marginal public service system, and getting the sort of ratings you would expect for arty English programmes and being talked about in Greenwich Village lofts. ABC, CBS and NBC would not touch them with a barge pole. *The Forsyte Saga* may have sold around the globe but you don't seriously imagine, do you, that it was seen by the sort of numbers that watch *I Love Lucy* or even *Coronation Street* – and nobody is suggesting you need a precious duopoly to make soap opera, are they?

As for the awards dished out in Venice or at black-tie dinners in New York, they look very good in the office foyer, but all they prove is that middlebrow broadcasters in Britain and Italy and the US share one lot of tastes while average Joes sitting down in front of sets all over the world to relax with *Dallas* share another, totally different lot.

It is all very well, they would add, to produce the television equivalent of *The Times* or even the *Daily Mail* but television is the biggest mass medium of all time and whether you happen to like it or not what the largest number of people actually want is the equivalent of the *Sun*. There is no point in arguing about it: we know it from every other mass medium and even television itself has proved it. Look what happened when ITV first started and provided a lightweight alternative after all those years when the BBC had been doing whatever its intellectual staff liked: ITV promptly took 70 per cent of the audience. Look at the ratings today, they tell you what the majority of people want. What right does your snooty duopoly have to stop them having it whenever they want it?

Of course, they would say, Britain has always posed as a democracy but it's really an oligarchy and the people in the BBC and ITV have got a vested interest in seeing that that is maintained in their business. Although you pretend to believe in democracy everybody knows quite well that the wishes of the majority can safely be ignored in Britain and the desires of the oligarchy preserved. You only have to look at capital punishment or immigration; everyone has known for years what the public wants but it doesn't make any difference, the law is decided by the 5 per cent of middle-class opinion formers not by the majority of ordinary people.

There's nothing special about the way that British television is organized to suit the tastes of a small élite; you've got a huge state apparatus specially constructed to see that things are organized like that. What sort of a democracy is it which makes poor people pay taxes to support an Arts Council to give millions of pounds to Covent Garden to subsidize opera tickets for the rich? With that sort of thing being done by the Government it's not very surprising that ITV can get away with paying more attention to beating the BBC at the BAFTA awards than to serving the audience they started out to please. Even with a mass medium like television you can safely ignore the preferences of the majority so long as you ban people like us who plan to give the public what they want.

'Duopoly' is just the sort of fancy name you would expect from a cartel of middle-class bureaucrats whose aim is to make pretentious programmes for people like themselves. In a real democracy like the USA where poor people aren't taxed to subsidize rich people's pastimes and they take notice of public attitudes your duopoly wouldn't last five minutes: the public wouldn't stand for it.

Incidentally, these hard-nosed businessmen would add, even supposing that highbrow prestige programmes are important, there's no proof that they can only be produced by your delicate duopoly. The British have clearly got a flair for television just as the Italians have a flair for restaurants and it's not going to disappear overnight simply because you do away with some outdated government regulations. On the contrary, more diversity will provide more opportunities for more programme-makers, just as Channel 4 already has. Bringing independent production houses into the business in response to the opening of Channel 4 hasn't driven standards down or reduced the number of prestige programmes, has it? It's pushed standards up and increased the number.

By the way, they would say approaching the end of their spiel, you do have to go to Channel 4 these days, or occasionally BBC 2, to find these famous prestige programmes, don't you, because in spite of what your supercilious duopolists like to pretend, the schedules on ITV and BBC 1 are looking more and more like the schedules on American television which they're so hoity-toity about. Have you counted the number of game shows on ITV recently? Did you notice the fight between these gentlemanly duopolists for the right to show *Dallas* which they all despise so much? With BBC1 so willing to prostitute themselves by using chat shows and soap opera and quizzes and American series to maximize their ratings how come they go on pretending to be Penelope Pure? They're fighting with all the commercial stuff so why not sell commercials?

'Don't get us wrong,' say the people with the shiny new equipment, putting their hands on their hearts, 'we don't want to close down the BBC or even take away their licence fee and make them live in the real world. We are not asking you to change the IBA or the ITV companies either. Let them carry on exactly as they are. All we want is the chance to compete. You don't have scarcity of wavelengths as an excuse to keep us out any more, we don't need wavelengths, just let us in with these reels of cable and these satellite dishes and we'll see if the public wants what we have to offer. If they don't then we'll fail, won't we, and you'll be none the worse off, and if we succeed it will prove that the public does want what we're offering. How can you be opposed to that?'

It is not an argument entirely without force (nor entirely without cunning since it seeks to blacken the duopolists as both too highbrow and too lowbrow) and it clearly has its adherents within the Thatcher Government. They would happily allow the people with the new technologies to have a go in the hope that their efforts in light entertainment might serve to bump-start the Information Revolution and hasten the coming of the wired society. The people in the BBC and ITV know this and their first response is to point warningly at Canada and Italy. 'You may have your doubts about us,' they say, 'but look at what actually happens to countries that have had good public service systems when you de-regulate and allow commercial competition in.'

The Canadian example is the best known because Canadian television, thanks to the country's geographical position and its largely English-speaking population, was one of the first to experience the full force of 'American cultural imperialism'. If you go back to 1970 and consider a Canadian city such as Calgary you find that only two television services were available: the public service network CBC, modelled on the BBC, and the commercial network CTV. They were splitting the audience 43:57 between them. Seven years later three-quarters of Calgary homes were connected to cable and the audience was split among ten networks. Of these, six were American and were attracting 29 per cent of the viewers. CTV still had the largest audience share though it had fallen to 37 per cent, and CBC's share had dropped to $15\frac{1}{2}$ per cent. (I am indebted to Timothy Hollins' highly detailed book *Beyond Broadcasting: Into the Cable Age*, BFI Publishing, 1984, for the Canadian statistics.) Nor should it be assumed that CTV's programmes were all Canadian; on the contrary, they were buying heavily from the US like practically every other network in the world.

Despite tremendous efforts by the Canadian Government with both sticks and carrots, attempts to preserve a high level of Canadian content in Canadian television have largely failed. Even though Canada did not de-regulate entirely but maintained rules about levels of Canadian-produced content and introduced tax concessions to make home production attractive, all they proved was that you can take a horse to water but you can't make it drink; the Canadian content was there but the Canadians chose not to watch it. By 1982 nearly three-quarters of all English-language viewing time was spent watching American programmes transmitted either by Canadian networks or direct by the Americans themselves. Of the drama viewed in Canada – films, soap operas, detective stories and serious plays – 96 per cent was foreign, most being American though some was British.

Italy's experience has been even more dramatic because even more swift. In 1976, completely unexpectedly, the Italian Constitutional Court ruled that the state broadcasting service Radiotelevisione Italiana, RAI, did not have a broadcasting monopoly as had always been assumed, but only a monopoly on broadcasting *nation-wide*: commercial stations were legal so long as they were local. Hundreds of stations promptly sprang up, broadcasting from the tops of high office blocks in every major Italian city. Some did little more than read out the news from the paper and invite good-looking women to come in and play strip poker in front of the cameras for very small prizes, a seemingly hopeless idea which proved an astonishing success, so strong, it seems, is the desire to appear on television. Strip quiz games followed.

But at the other end of the business spectrum several rich entrepreneurs began to bypass the 'local only' rule by opening stations or getting control of affiliates in different areas, then buying popular American programmes and sending out identical pre-recorded cassettes to be transmitted simultaneously. They were not broadcasting nation-wide but the effect was indistinguishable; *de facto* commercial networks had been constructed.

In June 1984 Brenda Maddox, editor of *The Economist*'s newsletter on world communications, 'Connections', wrote:

> It takes a trip to Italy to realize what non-regulation means. No rules. No rules at all – on pornography, on advertising, on political broadcasts. Italy's 600 private television stations simply show what they want – and the Italian public loves them. Viewers are deserting the three channels of the state television service, R A I, and the mutterings are increasing: 'Why should we pay the licence fee when we never watch the channels?' A poll in the Italian news weekly *Panorama* showed that the number of viewers who thought the licence fee unfair had risen from 33 to 43 per cent over two years and that if there were a referendum to abolish it 62 per cent would be in favour.

In autumn 1984, judges ordered the *de facto* commercial networks to be closed down on the grounds that they were not 'local' but by then they were regularly attracting more than half the national audience in peak viewing hours. The Italian public who, like the rest of the world, had grown fond of *Dallas* and *Dynasty* protested. Advertisers who had earmarked $500 million for commercial television that year protested. In the end the politicians had to back down and put the commercial stations back on the air under an interim decree. By 1985 the commercial stations were screening 75 per cent American content, and although R A I's ratings were recovering slightly one of their top executives, Claudio G. Fava, warned, 'We started out like the BBC but we risk ending up like PBS.'

The lesson drawn from Canada and Italy by Britain's partners in duopoly is that if you allow a *Sun*-style television service to come into existence it will not coexist peacefully with *Times*- or *Daily Mail*-style services even if its organizers want it to: it will rapidly kill them. The reasons for this have little to do with malice and much to do with economics and statistics. Neither the BBC nor ITV believes that there has ever been such a thing as a television network equivalent just to *The Times* since such an organization could not survive. Under a commercial system a service which limited itself to *TV Eye*, *The South Bank Show*, *Disappearing World* and similar minority programmes would never last because it would not attract enough advertising to support it. Similarly a public service network sticking to *Newsnight*, *Horizon* and *Shakespeare* would attract such relatively low ratings that no government would vote it a licence fee.

Such programmes have been sustained in Britain, the duopolists maintain, by being produced within the protective surroundings of the BBC and ITV which endeavour to be all things to all men: not just *The Times* but the *Sun* and the *Daily Mail* at the same time; not just *Weekend World* but *Crossroads* and *Minder* all within one service; not just *Horizon* but *Wogan* and *Grandstand*. You could say that the more popular programmes subsidize the more specialized ones. If you de-regulate television, they warn, and permit the men now standing in the wings to start networks which have neither a public service commitment nor government rules, then they will indeed provide an electronic equivalent of the *Sun*, with *Star Trek* and *Gun Law*, *Starsky and Hutch* and *I Love Lucy* running one after the other. This, they insist, is inevitable because the only stockpile of English-language programmes available to the new men is the American stockpile. Certainly the schedule of Rupert Murdoch's satellite Sky Channel, which can already be received in a few British cities on Rediffusion and Visionhire cables dating from the fifties which have been 'upgraded', seems to bear out this argument. The chief offerings in mid evening are almost all high-rated American and Australian series made some years ago: *Vegas*, *Fantasy Island*, *Charlie's Angels*, and so on.

And if you allow them to run a service of that sort, say the duopolists, then it will indeed attract huge ratings. The effect will be similar to that of ITV on the BBC in 1957 though more extreme. In order to survive, the BBC and ITV will have to fight with similar weapons, higher quality series will first be forced to the margins and then in a vicious circle as they lose viewers owing to their marginalized exposure they will be dropped. More will mean worse and Gresham's Law will ensure that bad drives out good. That is the dire warning from both BBC and ITV whose leaders have begun to speak with remarkable unanimity as they await the approach of the common enemy.

CHAPTER TEN

Oh Beautiful for Spacious Skies

Clearly there is a possibility that the global advance of television technology will bring in its wake multinational television operators whose activities will have effects similar to those of existing multinationals in the car and computer industries: the products on offer will be manufactured with care to suit the largest possible number of consumers around the world, or anyway to offend as few as possible, so that hundreds of millions will be pretty well satisfied but choice will be more limited than hitherto because the multinationals, whether by chance or design, will stifle smaller idiosyncratic national production. You could say that this is already happening, that *Dallas* is the Ford Sierra of television. The duopolists would argue that we have too many examples already for there to be any doubt about it. As long ago as 1983 Aubrey Singer, then Managing Director of BBC Television, said:

> The worry is simply this, that if American cable programming is going to be the way out for the British cable operator or, alternatively, if the British cable operator is going to lean heavily on plentiful second-hand Hollywood products, then our television screens are going to be a jumble of services without sense, meaning or national pride. Our country will become like Canada, assaulted by a multiplicity of mediocre foreign programming. Preserving the heartland implies fending off the invader and encouraging our indigenous production industry, which in turn

would be in danger of playing less and less part in the national life ...
The Canadianization of Britain is the greatest threat of all.

What this argument ignores is the fact that the so-called 'assault'
on Canada only succeeded because Canadian viewers chose in their
millions to watch American programmes in preference to those
offered by Mr Singer's counterparts in CBC. The Canadian people
did not merely encourage the assault, they demanded it. In a poll 81
per cent voted for unregulated access to American television and
many of those living in areas served only by Canadian television
spent thousands of dollars on satellite dishes in order to pick up
American programmes. In Britain there will be no need to 'preserve
the heartlands' of British broadcasting unless British viewers switch
voluntarily away from those heartlands once they are offered the
choice. The argument 'We can hang on to the heartlands of broadcasting just so long as you prevent anybody offering the viewers anything
they'd rather watch' carries precious little weight, especially when
you remember the mixture of soap opera, quizzes and American
programmes which the duopoly is already so busily exploiting.

Britain has always been generous in and rich from its cultural
assimilation, whether in orchestral music, drama, painting, literature, jazz or other forms of expression. We have welcomed and
lionized the work of Beethoven and Brahms, Ibsen and Ionesco,
Tolstoy and Turgenev, Basie and Bechet. Nobody suggested erecting
tariff barriers against them, let alone raising a poll tax to finance
studiously 'British' bodies with the aim of producing mountains of
home product designed to hold back the foreign rubbish. It does not
seem to worry us unduly that most of the classical music played in
Britain is 'foreign', as is most of the jazz, much of the painting in our
galleries, and so on. What on earth would be the point of protecting
a national culture within television if the nation's citizens cared so
little about it that, given half a chance, they switched over to
somebody else's?

The difference, of course, between those older media of expression
and television is that however great the popularity of a Beethoven or
a Bechet, young musicians coming along behind them can still reach

the public, be heard, and acquire a reputation if they are any good. The same goes for writers of books and plays and for painters of pictures. But television, thanks to its technology, operates on such a scale that the same is not true for ambitious young programme-makers. The genius in a garret who paints a picture can reach his public by hanging his work on the Hyde Park railings but his brother who makes a television programme needs a transmitter network or a communications satellite before he can reach an audience.

The real threat to the British duopoly is the extraordinary determination of the Americans to please as many people as possible as often as possible (though listening to the Pastoral Symphony one does wonder whether Beethoven was really all that different). When that deeply democratic principle – or demotic principle if that is the way you see it – operates within a free market, then there is always the possibility that American television thanks to its sheer size will indeed overwhelm everybody else's, especially in English-speaking countries. It may be that in the twenty-first century American culture will be as dominant in Britain as Roman culture was in the first century, although declaring that this will definitely be so on the grounds of Canada's experience seems somewhat hasty. Canada as a young community of immigrants sharing the world's longest land border with the USA can scarcely be considered an ideal model from which to predict possible British experience. Nor has the fluid situation in Italy proved much either way yet: at the time of writing, RAI, which had anyway retained half the viewers, was winning more of them back with Italian programming.

In any case, before falling hook, line and sinker for the argument dangled before us with such desperate eagerness by the BBC and ITV that our fellow countrymen (not you or I, perish the thought, but *they*) are going to be seduced on to a diet of American rubbish, it is worth asking whether everything about the American television business is really as unutterably appalling as the protectors of the duopoly would have us believe. Their own shamelessly enthusiastic exploitation of American programmes would seem to suggest otherwise.

BBC and ITV people are always keen to emphasize how small is the proportion of foreign (and by foreign they mean overwhelmingly American) programming on British television, about 14 per cent on all channels they say. Periodic counts have shown that while that figure may be accurate it is also misleading since it is worked out as a percentage of all the hours the transmitters are open whereas American programmes are usually shown when most viewers are available to see them. If you add up the number of hours in a week when the bulk of the audience is available to watch television – say between about 7.00 p.m. and midnight on weekdays and from 2.00 p.m. until midnight at weekends making a total of 45 hours a week – and then add up the American material during that time, you find the percentage is much nearer 34 per cent. Analysis of the week 15–21 December 1982 for instance shows 12 hours on BBC 1 (26.6 per cent) and 16½ hours (36.6 per cent) on ITV in the London region, which may have differed from other areas but only slightly.

One of the reasons American programmes are immensely popular with British broadcasters (despite hostile attitudes) is that they are so cheap. American production houses habitually budget to cover their costs and make a profit in their home market alone so that all the revenue from foreign sales is a bonus. Consequently they can sell very cheaply. Even after the absurd brouhaha over *Dallas*, in which Thames Television agreed to pay nearly double the previous price to get the series away from the BBC, they were still only paying £54,000 an episode. Compare that with other costs at the same date: £300,000 an episode to make *The Price* in England and Ireland, or £211,000 an hour to make BBC's *Juliet Bravo*, remembering that *Dallas* won bigger ratings than either. Moreover *Dallas* was at the very top of the price range; old American situation comedies, quizzes and soap operas could be bought for as little at £600 an hour, a price at which British producers would have difficulty keeping a studio on stand-by with the lights switched off.

Yet the BBC and ITV do not only use cheap American programmes as fillers for the extremities of the schedules, though certainly they do that. They also exploit the more popular series as key building-blocks in their peak-time schedules. Years ago the managing director of one of I T V's Big Five admitted to me, 'British television rode to success on the back of American programmes; it's been a matter of buying ratings while making our own prestige', and nothing much has changed. In the spring of 1985 BBC 1 was using *Dynasty* as its keystone programme between 8.05 and 8.50 p.m. on Saturday nights. *Fame* was serving the same purpose on Mondays and *Starsky and Hutch* on Fridays. The same channel was using *Dr Kildare* on Tuesdays and Thursdays to start its early evening build and on Sundays its schedules began and finished with American series: *Bonanza* started the evening and *Night Court* ended it. During the same period I T V was winning audiences with *The A-Team*, *T. J. Hooker*, *Magnum*, *Wanted Dead or Alive*, *Quincy* and *Knight Rider*. In one week BBC 2 was showing *The Rockford Files*, *Bilko* and five American films, about the same number as each of the other channels. Channel 4, despite the repeated claim of its Chief Executive, Jeremy Isaacs, that 'We are asked not for more of the same but for something different', was offering *The Cosby Show*, *The Addams Family* (a very cheap American comedy indeed, being twenty years old) and *Mean Streets* all on one evening. On other days Channel 4 offered *The Mary Tyler Moore Show*, *Newhart*, *My World and Welcome to It* and *Bewitched* (another cheapie from the sixties).

There is, furthermore, another huge category of programmes which although supposedly 'British' actually consists almost entirely of British-format versions of American series, many of them amazingly old: the game shows. In 1984 there was tremendous huffing and puffing from British critics and commentators about the appearance of a 'new' game show called *The Price Is Right* launched by Central TV. It was, said the protestors, objectionably American in the way it appealed to the mercenary instincts of its participants and whipped up hysteria among the studio audience. This American feel was hardly surprising since *The Price Is Right* was launched in the USA by Mark Goodson and Bill Todman, the world's most prolific and successful creators and adaptors of game shows, in 1956. It had been running there ever since and Central's version was merely a carbon copy produced under licence.

Goodson and Todman were responsible for *What's My Line?* which they started on American television in 1950. When the Americans finally abandoned it in 1975 it was described as 'hoary with age' yet in 1984 Thames TV brought it back to British screens for the third time. It has all the hallmarks of an ideal game show: it is supremely simple (the panel try to guess the occupations of the challengers and the identity of a celebrity guest), it can attract huge audiences (Gilbert Harding was featured in Madame Tussaud's Waxworks in the nineteen-fifties as 'The Most Famous Person In Britain' thanks to his irascible performances during the first BBC version of the show) and best of all it is clearly wondrously cheap. The price of a whole season of *What's My Line?* must be less than the cost of a single episode of *The Jewel in the Crown*. No wonder television never feels it has too many game shows.

According to Mark Goodson, in 1984 Goodson-Todman Productions alone had a dozen games running on British television: *Beat the Clock*, *Blankety Blank*, *Blockbusters*, *Call My Bluff*, *Play Your Cards Right*, *Child's Play*, *Family Fortunes*, *Top Secret*, *Now You See It*, *The Price Is Right*, *Tell the Truth* and *What's My Line?*

So much for protecting the British heartlands and all those dire warnings about the mindless American rubbish with which the new technologies will bombard us if we do not resist their approach. The most breathtaking example of this sort of hypocrisy is probably the BBC's pose of outrage at the prospect of 'wall-to-wall *Dallas*!' given that they were the very people who brought *Dallas* to Britain and who exploited it so skilfully for years to win their highest ratings. No doubt they would widen their eyes and protest that it was not *Dallas* they objected to but the wall-to-wall nature of its use by their would-be competitors, but then the concept of 'wall-to-wall *Dallas*' was a BBC invention, and not something that had actually been offered by any cable or satellite operator.

It is instructive to look at what the Americans actually produce rather than what British broadcasters in need of a bogyman like to pretend they produce. Certainly there are areas where British programmes tend to be better: drama adaptations of major novels (*Bleak House*, *The Pallisers*), blockbuster documentary series (*The World at War*, *Life on Earth*), arts programmes (*The South Bank Show*, operas), education and children's programmes. But there are also areas, significantly the more popular areas, in which the Americans tend to be better: filmed action drama (*Kojak*, *The Rockford Files*), news, sport, breakfast television, and, most of the time, situation comedies.

There was a brief period during the sixties when the British led the way in sitcom and *Steptoe and Son* and *Till Death Us Do Part* were successfully Americanized as *Sanford and Son* and *All in the Family*. Later *Man about the House* became *Three's Company*. But British broadcasters went on living on those laurels for an embarrassingly long time. Go back beyond the sixties and you find the Americans making *Bilko* and *I Love Lucy*, not just the two most popular comedy series the world has ever seen but two of the best. At the top of her form Lucille Ball was an unmatched comedienne and Phil Silvers' superb series as Bilko, the scheming master sergeant, has been the most influential comedy in the whole history of television: his techniques can be seen in the work of virtually every subsequent leading television comedian from Eric Morecambe to Alan Alda. Nor did the superiority of Britain's 'socially aware' sitcoms of the sixties last very long; the Americans rapidly leapfrogged the British series to make *Maude*, *M.A.S.H.* and *Mary Hartman, Mary Hartman*. In the eighties they were sending us *Rhoda*, *Soap*, *Taxi* and *Cheers*, and we were sending them *Benny Hill*. Which way does that suggest the rubbish was travelling?

Anyone who has stayed even a short time in the US knows that the American breakfast shows are considerably better than their British imitators. Admittedly in terms of content that is not difficult, and admittedly the American shows were pretty poor for an awfully long time. But at least the American system meant that the big networks were able to use their news infrastructure to support and enrich their breakfast programmes while they slowly built audiences.

In Britain that is true of the BBC (though the style of *Breakfast Time* with bluff Frank Bough in his woolly cardigan, Selina Scott dropping her clangers, and a fat astrologer reading 'your stars' has been, to say the least, unfortunate), but desperately untrue of ITV.

Had the IBA had the sense to give its breakfast contract to ITN, then Britain might quickly have acquired a service to match that of the better American breakfast programmes. Since ITN is financed by the ITV companies the early money problems would not have been disastrous, and since ITN is one of the world's best television news outfits the basis of a high-grade breakfast service would have been there from the start. As it is, Britain's commercial breakfast show with its endless low-grade chit-chat has been far worse than all the ghastly scenarios which the duopolists keep painting to show what we will get from the new technologies if we are not jolly careful.

Nor is breakfast the only time when American viewers are offered better programmes than their British counterparts. American network news is by and large superior to Britain's, thanks to more money, more resources, more time, and a less inbred and nationalistic approach. Some regular American daytime shows are better than any comparable series in Britain, for instance the morning series *Phil Donahue*, a discussion programme with guests and audience participation, run with tremendous verve and intelligence by its host who happily takes on anything from international politics to the morality of striptease.

The British belief that American viewers do much worse when it comes to single drama is not only complacent but somewhat inaccurate. Certainly the single play has declined in American television faster and further than in Britain but the TV movie genre is stronger in the US than the UK, and not all TV movies are meretricious nonsense. American TV movies from the eighties such as *Adam*, concerned with child kidnapping, and *Something About Amelia*, which managed to deal sanely with incest in a programme aimed at a mass audience, are as powerful and as important if not as strikingly well produced as those British works from the sixties such as *Cathy Come Home* or *The Lump*. For some reason they often receive no showing in Britain. When it comes to the biggest topic of all, the bomb, it was the BBC which suppressed the British drama (*The War Game*) in the mid sixties and the Americans who made and showed *The Day After* in 1983. Only after that were British audiences offered a BBC drama on the same theme, *Threads*, followed by a major documentary on the same subject, *On the Eighth Day*.

As for the showing of *Threads* and *On the Eighth Day* in the US, were they banished to the margins of television on the Public Broadcasting Service? On the contrary, they were beamed across the nation via satellite by 'SuperStation WTBS' for cable delivery on successive nights at 8.00 p.m., bang in the middle of prime time; not quite what you might expect if you believed all the 'wall-to-wall *Dallas*' stories about cable told by Britain's duopolists. SuperStation WTBS is a mixed content service run from Atlanta by Ted Turner, the man responsible for America's excellent twenty-four-hour Cable News Network (CNN). By spring 1985 CNN had 17 million cable subscribers in the US and was planning to extend the service to Britain and western Europe later in the year using the Intelsat V satellite.

Most noticeably, of course, the Americans have always been superior in the field of popular filmed adventure series, a genre which the British manage to master comparatively rarely. Practically all the notable and cherishable British exceptions of recent years – *The Sweeney, Minder, Widows, Fox, Out* – have been made by Euston Films, a small commercial offshoot of Thames Television. The American tradition in this field goes back beyond television to the cinema, and a clear line can be traced from the work of men such as D. W. Griffith with whose words this book begins, to *Hill Street Blues* which, with its broad canvas and hectic pace, is not as unlike *Birth of a Nation* or *Intolerance* as it might at first seem.

After the great age of American cinema in the thirties and forties when so many of the best cowboy and crime movies were made, television came into this area in the fifties with series such as *Gunsmoke* and *Dragnet*, and the subsequent list has become almost endless, whether in westerns (*Rawhide*, *Alias Smith and Jones*), crime (*Naked City*, *The Untouchables*), science fiction (*The Outer Limits*, *The Twilight Zone*), private-eye series (*Columbo*, *Baretta*), medical series (*Ben Casey*, *Dr Kildare*) or fantasy (*Six Million Dollar Man*, *The Bionic Woman*).

The widespread British assumption that such series are slickly made, mindless rubbish simply does not stand up to even the briefest serious critical analysis. Naturally the genre varies; of course the worst moments in *Star Trek* have been hilariously awful, but the best episodes of *The Rockford Files* have been superb: the production values (location, costumes, props) are as high as you would find anywhere in the world, the acting is consistently good from the star (James Garner) through to the smallest bit-part player, and the scripts leave those in most comparable British series looking flat-footed, slow and dull.

In recent years, moreover, although some of the American offerings in this category have become increasingly absurd, violent and escapist – *The Dukes of Hazzard*, *The A-Team* or *Knight Rider* for instance – other series have contrived to combine gripping entertainment with a remarkably honest awareness and analysis of the major problems of the modern world. *Lou Grant* was not only one of the most entertaining (and incidentally most realistic) series ever made about newspapermen, it also dealt head-on with alcoholism, the Vietnam war, sexual abuse of children and a host of other touchy subjects. In Britain you have to go back to 1960 and *Z-Cars* to find a similar combination realized with such power and style. In the US during the seventies and eighties such semi-comedy series as *Taxi*, *Barney Miller* and *Cheers* have dealt with problems of immigration, with the growth of feminism, with modern crime and so on as well as providing entertainment of a sort which is enjoyed by hundreds of millions of viewers around the world.

The air of innate superiority adopted by so many British broadcasters whenever the subject of American television comes up looks very odd indeed when you consider the excellence of series such as *Hill Street Blues*. Growing partly out of habits and ideas which were tested in *Kojak* and *Lou Grant*, *Hill Street Blues* combines pace, drama, a multiplicity of interleaved plots, ensemble acting, finely judged comedy which draws its strength from truth (often looking like farce but never feeling like it), and an almost embarrassing willingness to face up to America's modern problems – the gun laws, chaotic sexual morality, drugs, and many others. None of Britain's early attempts to 'do a *Hill Street*' in series such as *The Bill* and *The Practice* came even close to achieving the speed or richness of the original.

It is unfortunately true that some of the bravest and best of American series in recent years have been brought to an end in shameful circumstances: *Lou Grant* and *Soap* were both scrapped after endless caterwauling by a noisy minority of small-minded viewers who like to call themselves the silent or moral majority. That is one of the penalties of a free market such as the USA's where commercial undertakings are open to political and moral pressures and in which the executives lack the strength of character of their programme-makers. On the other hand it is also true that if you live in New York City today and subscribe to Manhattan Cable you can find an openness and freedom in dealing with religious, political, sexual and social matters which you would never find anywhere within Britain's vaunted duopoly.

There is one other factor to take into account when considering American programmes: their true quality is often obscured in their home country because of the appalling frequency and obtrusiveness of the commercials. It is virtually standard American practice to run the first advertising break immediately after the opening credits, hence the habit of putting a 'sting' on the front of the programme to alert the viewers and tempt them to stay tuned through the first break. What is more, whereas commercial broadcasters in Britain are obliged to make a clear distinction between programme and advertisement (the transition usually consists nowadays of the appearance of the programme's title and then a fade to black), American broadcasters run straight from the programme into the ads. Thus the experience of watching television in the USA is not only different from the experience of watching BBC television in Britain, it is even different from watching British commercial television.

One of the most significant consequences is that large numbers of Americans have been eager to take up offers of pay-television of one sort or another if it gives them access to programmes, especially movies, without commercials. When attempts are made to use American experience as a base from which to predict the likely 'take-up rate' for new pay-television systems in Britain it is vital to remember that British viewers already have a commercial system which subjects them to fewer breaks, and a BBC system which uses no breaks at all within programmes though the Corporation does, of course, run some of the most polished and professional advertisements between programmes, all promoting the BBC's own material.

CHAPTER ELEVEN

T V Pilms and Cinema Flays

Whenever the future of television is discussed, whether by bankers or critics, broadcasters or politicians, Americans or Europeans, there is one form which begins to dominate the conversation sooner or later, and usually sooner: movies. There are still Britons who blanch at the very word, objecting that it is an Americanism, but no other term will do because the only synonym, 'film', has far too many other meanings: 'How many films did you take in Torremolinos?' 'Did you see that film of the Prime Minister on the news last night?' Everybody knows that a movie is something which was made for the cinema, lasts about ninety minutes and, with luck, stars Charles Laughton or Greta Garbo.

It seems odd at first that a form which began attracting queues outside the Lumière brothers' Cinématographe in the nineteenth century should still be considered central, even vital, to the future of mass entertainment when we are fast approaching the year 2000 and some of us are already receiving our evening entertainment from other continents via space satellites. Yet the continued pulling power of movies is beyond question; other things being equal (time of day, strength of alternative offerings) an old movie on television will almost invariably prove more popular than any but the most successful of television's own programmes. Examples can be found in any month of any year, and just one will do: when BBC 1 scheduled

Dirty Harry starring Clint Eastwood on a Monday night in February 1985 at 10.05 p.m., playing against *Arena* and *Newsnight* on BBC 2, *News at Ten* and a Frank Sinatra movie on ITV, and *Newhart* and *Pictures of Poland* on Channel 4, it attracted 14.85 million viewers and reached No. 7 in the week's national Top 10 even though it had been shown on television umpteen times before.

The way that the cinema industry's own fortunes have declined in inverse proportion to the rise of television is indicated by the fact that the television audience for that single movie on that February evening was more than a quarter of the total UK cinema admissions for the whole of the previous year (55 nillion). The speed of the cinema's descent has been dramatic: in 1946 there were 1,635 million admissions. As recently as 1969 Britain had 1,559 cinema sites and annual admissions were 215 million. Ten years later the number of sites had fallen to 978 (though the number of screens had remained stable, this being the period when proper cinemas were being broken down into several poky little rooms) and admissions had almost halved to 112 million. Since then the deterioration has been even faster. An opinion poll in 1984 taken among heads of households and housewives showed that 63 per cent never went to the cinema at all. British movie production has also slipped rapidly: in 1972 more than 100 features were registered for theatrical release; by 1977 the figure was down to 51; and by 1982 it had halved again to 24.

There have been rational, realistic and even-toned reactions to this catalogue of decline from cinema people such as David Puttnam, Simon Perry and ... well, David Puttnam. Unfortunately their sane comments have too often been lost beneath a cacophony set up by the two more familiar groups within the industry: those who favour blustering conceit and the others who believe in whining self-pity. The first group wait for the slightest sign of success from a British movie, see that it is showered with awards, and then start screaming like Mohammed Ali declaring that Britain always was the greatest, and is about to be again – so long as there are bigger handouts of public money for the film industry. The second group pumps out great waves of reports by way of little magazines and endless committees complaining about how beastly television is because it pays peanuts for old movies and then uses them to steal away the cinema's rightful audiences. This is followed by a whine about public handouts to the film industry in Britain being too small compared with those in Peru or Australia or whichever country is currently making a desperate bid to become a movie-makers' tax haven.

One of the whiners' favourite ploys is to point to the much better survival records of French, Italian and German cinema and argue that this has occurred because regulations in those countries protect the film industry and ensure that movies reach television later, less often, and more expensively than in Britain. It is a dishonest argument since it ignores the US where cinema has survived even more successfully despite there being no protective regulations whatsoever. In 1984 there were 18,800 cinema screens in the US, a 10 per cent increase over 1977, and admissions rose to 1.2 billion: an average of 5.5 visits a year per head of the population compared to fewer than 1 per head in Britain. No doubt one reason for the disparity is explained by the saying that 'British cinema is alive and well and called television'. British cinema has always tended towards the domestic scale rather than the grand sweep of Hollywood, with Britons such as David Lean clearly being the exception rather than the rule. The talent which in America, France, Italy and Germany has gone into the cinema in the last thirty years has been much more likely in Britain to go into television, which is so well suited to the domestic scale. While French cinema had its new wave, Italian cinema its post-war renaissance, and German cinema its upthrust of new realism, Britain had a golden age in television. (Or, to be fair, very largely in television. There were half a dozen movies in the sixties – *Room at the Top*, *This Sporting Life*, *Saturday Night and Sunday Morning* and so on – which arguably formed a British cinema renaissance, however miniature and short-lived.)

There is one other crucial reason why the film industry has declined so much faster in Britain than elsewhere: the only thing to have kept pace with the rising cost of UK cinema seats has been the rising level of unpleasantness associated with every other aspect of a cinema visit. While Continental cinemas tend to be expensive but luxurious and American cinemas comparatively cheap and pleasant with good projection and sound systems and staff who want you to have a good time, the average British cinema is like a bad dream: a dim and scruffy building, bossy staff, no booking facilities, a perpetual battle between the smell of onions from the hot dogs and the reek of disinfectant, projection systems which are not just bad but studiously ignored, sound systems inferior to a domestic hi-fi, and an absolute determination on the part of the management to keep the real starting time of the film a secret. With the grand auditoriums of old broken down into a series of cubicles with Lilliputian screens, the entire experience is not unlike watching television in a public lavatory – at enormous expense.

That it is British cinemas and not British audiences which need jollying up is proved by two facts: when a hit movie such as *Star Wars* or *Chariots of Fire* comes along, the public flocks to see it in spite of the disgusting conditions; and when offered decent facilities as in London's relatively new Screen On The Green chain the public will become loyal and frequent enough visitors to make the business a success.

None of which is to deny that the main bulk of the mass audience which used to visit the cinema from fifty to a hundred times a year now watches television. When Britons flocked to the pictures in their millions in the nineteen-forties they did so because the cinema was warmer than their homes and it provided camaraderie at a time when it was needed, but above all there was nothing better or even half as good to do at home. That is no longer true. Homes are now generally warm, old movies can be seen on television for nothing, and fairly new movies can be seen on the VCR for a pound or two. In view of the film industry's self-propagating myths it is as well to emphasize that the greatest days of the cinema were over *before* 1955, but it is also fairly plain that once ITV arrived with its schedules aimed plumb at the centre of the mass market the picture palaces were in even greater trouble.

Sure enough, in thirty years the cinema audience has been reduced to a tiny rump, composed almost entirely of teenagers and young adults. But while television has taken the audience it has never succeeded in replacing movies. It is no mere coincidence that cinema-going, which required strangers to congregate in the dark in dream palaces, managed to create stars. Week after week unreal super-beings – Dietrich, Peck, Pickford, Fairbanks – created and re-created realms of fantasy, quite literally larger than life, into which the audience could willingly transport themselves and, for an hour or two, lose themselves. Television could hardly be more of a contrast: chattering away in a corner of the front room it is considerably smaller than life, it specializes not in fantasy but reality, it is watched casually by family groups with the lights on and often while they are doing something else such as eating or talking. Unsurprisingly it creates not larger-than-life stars but ordinary life-size domestic 'personalities'. When fans met Clark Gable they fainted, but when they meet Larry Grayson they poke him in the chest and say 'Shut that door!' Television celebrities such as Michael Aspel and Richard Baker (giants within their own world relatively speaking) are forever remarking that when viewers come upon them in the street they sincerely believe they are old acquaintances. The ethos of television seems simply incapable of creating anything as grand as a star.

Television nevertheless has to find some way of sustaining the supply of movies. To date the younger medium has done very nicely out of the older; occasionally television has paid as much for an old movie as £4.5 million, which was the BBC's successful bid against ITV in the 1981 auction of *Gone with the Wind*. (It came in a package with 55 other titles, but the others had all been shown on television before.) Two years earlier the Corporation paid £2 million for *The Sound of Music*. The argument justifying such huge prices has always been that the movies are sold – hired on licence for a limited period, actually – on the understanding that they can be transmitted several times, and since movies of this sort attract vast audiences the per-capita cost is very low. But such blockbusters are in any case the exceptions. The normal cost for old movies works out at an average of about £20,000 an hour which is less than a tenth of television's own costs for originating reasonable drama.

Unfortunately for the film industry, the businessmen in television (and this applies at least as much in public service organizations as in commercial television) take the attitude that while movies may be a bargain, and television could afford to pay more, just as the film industry would dearly like them to pay more, they are not going to. And however much some movie people may whine it seems pretty clear that nothing untoward is occurring: if a better return could be made by keeping the movies off television and showing them in the cinema, then that is precisely what would happen. Nobody forces the cinema industry to take television's money.

At first sight the coming of the new technologies far from representing a threat to the film industry seems to hold out the possibility of salvation. Virtually all the new hardware – cable, DBS, VCR, videodisc, HDTV – wants movies. The most successful of the new technology operators in the US is the satellite-to-cable movie channel Home Box Office (HBO) owned by Time Inc. It was the first in its field and proved conclusively that the public will pay considerable sums to receive new or recent movies in their homes. In 1984 HBO's profits fell from $150 million to $80 million but at that stage no other cable channel had even come into profit. It is universally accepted in the industry that if cable is ever to make any progress in Britain a movie channel will lead the way, and the same applies to DBS. Meanwhile VCR is already in one-third of Britain's homes and spreading movies as fast as the high-street rental companies can move them, or rather as soon as they are allowed to acquire them. In the US a clear pecking order for movie use has been established: the average new release is available exclusively to the cinema for the first six months, then it goes on to video cassette and videodisc, it becomes available after twelve months to pay-cable, after two and a half years the three big broadcast networks can buy it, and after five years local television (for which there is no British equivalent) is allowed, in effect, to put it into repertory.

The surge in VCR sales in America and the strong American habit of movie rental rather than time-shifting had an almost immediate effect on Hollywood: 30 per cent more movies were started during the first three-quarters of 1984 than during the same period in 1983. Circumstances in Britain are rather different, but even here television's expansion has led to the commissioning of a considerable number of movies which would, almost certainly, not otherwise have appeared. From its inception in 1982 Channel 4 adopted a policy within its 'fiction' strand (a term carefully chosen to avoid the traditional preconceptions attached to 'drama') of commissioning and co-producing low-budget movies. For an outlay of about £6 million a year they are acquiring twenty or so 'films', as they call them, and transmitting them under the generic title *Film on Four*. Channel 4's senior commissioning editor David Rose has always been very pragmatic about how these works should reach the public: some such as *Moonlighting* have had six months or so in the cinema before appearing on Channel 4, some such as *Experience Preferred But Not Essential* have been premiered on television and then gone into the cinema, and one – *Those Glory Glory Days* – actually opened at exactly the same moment on the large and small screen.

The BBC has developed a strand of fiction modelled upon Channel 4's *Film on Four* which it calls *Screen Two*, though interestingly one of its strongest offerings in its early days was not made on film at all but on tape (Alan Clarke's powerful work *Contact* about a British Army patrol on the Irish border). There has also been a long-running campaign within the BBC to start a real movie department, shooting on 35mm film and creating work which is actually intended for theatrical release, the major difficulty being that the technical unions would then enforce the same demands and restrictions as they do upon real movie-production houses, conditions which are much tougher than those traditionally in force at the Corporation.

Those of us whose earliest passion was the cinema, and who mourned the passing of the great days when two or three new releases arrived in town every week, at first welcomed this upsurge of activity inspired by television. It looked as though the small screen was beginning to repay its debt to the large. Indeed it really seemed as though television, in the process of growing up, was not going to kill the film industry after all but on the contrary would provide a quite unexpected boon for the movie enthusiast. Although the new material was being produced largely for viewers who would watch on television screens it appeared to promise reinvigoration of the cinema in the process. From time to time every director longs to be able to sit among a cinema audience and feel the public reaction to his work, and on the marketing side of the television business there was a growing awareness of the disproportionate publicity value and prestige to be gained from theatrical showcasing even when the number of people seeing a work in the cinema would only be a tiny fraction of 1 per cent of the number eventually watching it on television. All the pressures were to produce works which could be shown equally well on large and small screen.

Sure enough, the number of ninety-minute filmed fiction productions has been on the increase; yet the more we see of them the clearer it becomes that we are not being given movies in the great tradition of cinema but, more often than not, hybrids combining some characteristics of television's single play with some characteristics of the old British cinema. Perhaps when you come down to it there is nothing very surprising about this. When Griffith directed *Intolerance* and Kubrick made *2001: A Space Odyssey* both men were clearly intensely aware of working for a luminescent canvas which would physically dominate its audience. The moment when the soldier falls from the castle wall in *Intolerance* and Griffith instantaneously narrows his golden-section rectangle to a thin, vertical shaft becomes meaningless because so tiny on television. In *Bad Day at Black Rock* John Sturges exploits his huge CinemaScope screen again and again to make those points about mankind and landscape which lie at the very heart of the movie; they are lost on the box. Unless your sitting-room is fitted with eight-track Dolby stereo sound you cannot begin to reproduce with television the electrifying effect achieved by George Lucas in the opening sequence of *Star Wars* as the star-ship thunders into shot from *behind* the audience. Watching Abel Gance's *Napoleon* in a cinema with a full orchestra as the director intended is a powerful and wholly engrossing experience, as those of us fortunate enough to be present in the Empire Leicester Square when Thames Television finally staged Kevin Brownlow's lovingly restored print know. Watching it on television is like listening to Beethoven's Ninth played on a mouth-organ; better than never hearing it at all, but a very poor second best. The only excuse for reducing such works by displaying them on television is that a lot of viewers will otherwise never be able to see them in any form.

What on earth would be the point of Britain's new young directors creating such material? While they may value the kudos attached to theatrical release they know that television is where the overwhelming majority of viewers will see their work. In any case most of them – people such as Richard Eyre, Mike Leigh, Stephen Frears and Karl Francis, directors respectively of *The Ploughman's Lunch*, *Four Days in July*, *Walter* and *Giro City* – clearly have no ambition whatsoever to transport their audiences into realms of fantasy peopled by larger-than-life stars. Quite the reverse. Virtually to a man they are concerned to bring us up against gritty reality depicted on a domestic scale, and the grittier the more realistic, and the more domestic the better.

There are some types of movie which do not rely for their impact upon the unique properties of cinema viewing. The Ealing comedies, the Warner Brothers black and white thrillers, the RKO musicals, and full-length animated cartoons are examples. They work perfectly well today on television, and yet nobody in television seems to be attempting to create modern equivalents. In some instances television does have somewhat similar forms of its own – the situation comedy and the police series for instance – but these are not really comparable, being series or serials and lacking both the budgets and the production values which contributed so much to the success of the one-off comedies, thrillers, musicals and cartoons made for the cinema.

Sadly it looks as though television will continue to expand and cinema to shrink until some sort of stasis is reached with, on the one hand, a number of specialized centres (more than at present) serving those cinéastes who want the sort of facilities provided by the

National Film Theatre; and on the other hand urban and, increasingly, suburban complexes showing Hollywood blockbusters tailored to the big screen and cinema sound (*Close Encounters of the Third Kind*, *A Passage to India*, *Superman XLVII*) and previewing work on a domestic scale shortly to be networked on national television. To be fair, not every television/movie hybrid falls into this category – *The Draughtsman's Contract* and *Angel* are examples of such co-productions which exhibit a powerful sense of cinema. But the more we see of this trend the more exceptional such works appear.

CHAPTER TWELVE

Acacia Avenue Syndrome

As we approach the crucial question – what should our attitude be towards television tomorrow? – there is one more major problem to be faced: although in terms of numbers television is the most popular mass medium the world has ever seen, in Britain it appears to have virtually no friends, or none with much influence. Politicians, press, lawyers, police, academics, clergy, the solid centre of the middle-class intelligentsia, all seem more or less inimical to television. There are those who actually work in the industry, of course, but even some of them take a remarkably supercilious attitude towards the business. Worse, there is a vested interest throughout the existing organizations on both sides of the duopoly in preserving the status quo: any innovation could represent a threat to what has so far been a very comfortable existence and consequently the attitude of both BBC and ITV towards new ideas tends to be: 'Either you let us do it ourselves or we oppose it.'

Politicians are on the whole suspicious of television; if they are not seeking to use its influence to their own ends, then they are fearful of the influence which they believe may be used against them. No doubt this is the chief reason why they have, so far, preserved greater control over broadcasting than over other mass media. One or two politicians who have worked in television (Austin Mitchell for instance and Geoffrey Johnson Smith) do champion its interests at

Westminster and from time to time it is even possible to find a Cabinet minister who is well disposed towards television as a whole: William Whitelaw has been a notable example. But their attitudes have been noticeable precisely because they are so exceptional; hostility is the rule.

This has been most obvious in the attitudes expressed over the years towards the idea of televising Parliament's own activities. Given that Parliamentary proceedings are public and that there is a public gallery in each House it would seem logical that the most popular mass medium of the day should be used to extend the public gallery into every elector's home. Yet time after time up to the spring of 1985 Parliamentarians voted against even experimental broadcasts. In public the reasons given usually involved the fear that Parliament would be misrepresented, an argument which became quite absurd after April 1978 when Parliamentary proceedings started to be broadcast live on radio, offering the public the worst of all possible worlds: all the sound and all the fury of Question Time with no pictures to show that what sounded like a vicious beargarden was usually no such thing.

In any case the 'misrepresentation' argument was largely hypocritical. What many MPs feared, as they admitted in private, was not that the cameras would lie but that they would tell the truth and show the front bench spokesmen with their feet up on the table, show the vast tiers of empty seats during most debates (voters would be much too stupid to understand about MPs working in committees elsewhere) and, worst of all, show how some Members behave during the vital period round about 10.00 p.m. when winding-up speeches and divisions take place after MPs have had dinner, in some cases a rather liquid meal enjoyed in one of Westminster's many bars. It is another example of the way television can shift power to the people: the medium can chisel away at the famous 'representative' nature of British democracy (meaning the freedom of MPs to do pretty much as they please once they get to Westminster with virtually no accountability between elections) by showing viewers what their representatives are up to, and that is altogether too Benn-ite for many Parliamentarians.

Furthermore, politicians could hardly miss the fact that however long they could keep their electors at arm's length by banning the cameras from Parliament, they could not prevent television becoming a more and more vital medium for political debate and their own chamber concomitantly less and less important. Hence their hostility towards television, ranging from guarded uncooperativeness to virulent aggression.

Much the same set of attitudes exists in Fleet Street. When television emerged as a commercial competitor to newspapers in 1955 the hostility was quite undisguised, the fear being that television advertising would drain revenue from the papers and destroy the national press. The Beaverbrook papers were particularly antagonistic, not only refusing to use the term 'Independent Television' but even eschewing 'commercial' and habitually employing instead the contemptuous phrase 'plug-TV', the reference of course being not to three-pin plugs but advertisers' plugs. Slowly attitudes have changed and in many editions nowadays the tabloid press devotes more space to television in one way or another – programme schedules, gossip about the stars, 'shock' stories about imminent personnel changes in soap operas – than to any other topic. Yet even now the tabloid press could scarcely be described as a friend of television: the relationship is increasingly parasitical with television used on the one hand to advertise bingo promotions and on the other hand to provide grist for the gossip mills.

Broadcasters often express puzzlement about the ambivalent way in which newspapers both exploit and vilify television and wonder why the same treatment is not meted out to other forms of expression and other mass media, quite missing the point, it seems, that while theatre and cinema and books pose virtually no threat to the press, television is a direct competitor which could eventually supplant most newspapers. Consequently although the outright opposition of the mid fifties has been replaced by a grudging accommodation there is still precious little love lost between them. The fact that the two

RMs – Rupert Murdoch and Robert Maxwell, owners of the *Sun* and the *Daily Mirror* respectively – are the two most important proprietors in Britain's nascent satellite and cable business, Murdoch having bought the Sky Channel and Maxwell the upgraded Rediffusion cable networks, should not necessarily be taken as an indication of any growing identity of interests between the people in the press and those in television. The electronic ventures of the two proprietors put one in mind of the shrewd stable owners of the late nineteenth century who continued to deal with horses but also stuck petrol pumps outside, just in case.

Lawyers and the police scarcely seem to be under any great threat from television, yet here too one frequently encounters attitudes of deep distrust. Television crews with their cameras are often accused, rightly no doubt, of being the reason for and not merely the recorders of illegal activities, ranging from minor civil disobedience by demonstrating students to major aircraft-hijacking by international terrorists. Some policemen and some lawyers have joined the 'clean up TV' bandwagon and blamed television for a huge range of crimes. In a single week in the spring of 1985 television was blamed for a rise in the number of cases of cruelty to animals investigated by the RSPCA – with Chief Inspector Charles Marshall declaring 'Television films and particularly videos are to blame; people, especially youngsters, seem to have developed the view that there's nothing much wrong with maltreating animals', as though television had invented bear baiting, fox hunting, cock fighting and hare coursing – and the judge in the 'Fox' rape trial referred to the supposed influence of sadistic sex videos in the case he was trying.

To be fair, other lawyers and other policemen have realized that it was not an addiction to *Starsky and Hutch* which sent Genghis Khan on his wicked way, that Torquemada did not need video nasties to give him his nasty ideas, and that if there is a connection between sadistic crime and sadistic programmes it is that those predisposed to enjoy the former will also be predisposed to enjoy the latter; that indeed the whole of recorded history shows that the absence of sadistic television does not by one iota reduce the incidence of sadistic crime. There does now seem to be a growing realization in legal circles that encouraging over-anxious people to blame television for the immemorial criminal and sadistic elements within human society is counter-productive in that it reduces the drive to look for the real causes and find preventive measures. The fact remains that television cannot look to the forces of law and order for very much friendship or support.

Academics and teachers, with a few exceptions such as the historian A. J. P. Taylor who proved to have a rare and astonishing gift for ad-libbing to camera, have tended to be almost as cool towards television as politicians. So have clergymen, again with occasional exceptions such as Don Cupitt. The objection here seems to be that television cheapens and over-simplifies their work, a feeling very close to the complaint heard so often from Acacia Avenue that 'Television makes things too easy.' Experience suggests that there is no point in arguing with those who hold such views since what they are expressing is not reasoned thought but folk myth of the sort that asserts that medicine is only effective if nasty.

For nearly two thousand years society has revered and rewarded those best able to master learning through reading and for the past five hundred years the printing press has been the central engine of knowledge. It is not difficult to imagine the outrage among bookish people if an ambitious young man in a publishing firm were promoted to department head today and declared, 'I'm not a child of the book age. Television comes first for me.' Yet when Alan Yentob was appointed Head of Arts and Music for BBC Television in spring 1985, a key post in the television world, no one batted an eyelid when he said, 'I'm not a child of the television age. Books come first for me.'

Many people raised in the book culture from the very nursery and educated for decades almost entirely by print become deeply offended when told that Johnny-Come-Lately television, barely fifty years old, is already outdoing books in some areas (wildlife, current affairs, education via satellite in illiterate Indian villages, for instance) and deeply anxious if told that, thanks to all sorts of audio-visual wonders, children today can often acquire knowledge with less effort than hitherto. The very idea of less effort seems to offend both the puritan conscience and the belief that 'They should go through the mill as we did.' It is a disturbing experience to have a conversation with a teacher who believes that all reading is 'better' than television because 'It involves activity rather than passivity' and to end by asking 'Are you seriously suggesting your ten-year-olds would benefit more from reading *Beano* because they have to turn the pages than from watching Attenborough's *Life on Earth* on television?' and to receive the screamed response 'Yes, I am, yes! Anything rather than bloody television!'

It is equally disturbing to listen to a roomful of historians all agreeing more or less strongly that television is innately misleading when it comes to history and that books are inherently superior. To the disinterested non-specialist it seems obvious that being misleading or not depends upon the historian, not the medium, and that while there are some things for which books are better (analysis of abstract thought, for instance) there are others for which television is better. No book can convey all the information contained in the tone of voice of an old IRA man remembering the uprising of Easter 1916 in *Ireland: A Television History*, or in the expression in the eyes of concentration camp survivors in *The World at War*. Books cannot match the vividness and immediacy of newsreel from the 1953 coronation or the American retreat from Saigon. But once again, whatever one feels ought to be the case, many historians and teachers remain hostile to television.

If one were looking for the extreme example of those who are clearly obsessed with television yet deeply guilty about watching it, the best place to start would surely be the Oxford senior common rooms. In the sixties when there was a surge in academic punditry and some vying between the dons to appear on the box, however much they might despise it, the story was told of the seething history professor whose colleagues had all made their appearances and who finally received the longed-for summons from the BBC in London. When told that the fee would be £50 he replied, 'That seems a bit steep but never mind, where shall I send it?' Among the dreaming spires today the medium often elicits the same combination of fascination and guilt-induced loathing. Here you find frequent recourse to the pathetic fallacy (Ruskin's phrase to describe the attribution of human feelings to inanimate objects) in the attempt to shift blame from the viewer's weak will-power on to the pretended 'power' of the television set.

The first chapter of the 1982 book *Television: The Medium and its Manners* by Peter Conrad, lecturer in English, is a classic example. The opening paragraph begins: 'In the Oxford college to which I belong, a television set has been supplied for the delectation of the brain-weary dons. It's hidden away in a musty chamber, bottling up the fug of defunct cigars, called the smoking room.' (What a sentence from a professor of English.) Later in the paragraph he explains: 'People sometimes scuttle across the quad after dark to watch it, conscious (in their furtiveness) that in doing so they're neglecting their pedagogic chores, *and the set they watch is as ashamed as they are.*' [My italics.] Later in the chapter Conrad declares, 'The box is no longer our guest, conscious (as in Red Skelton's goodbye) of being on probation. Now it imposes its schedules on us, and defines our reality according to its own convenience.' No doubt this power of the box to impose upon Mr Conrad explains why he watched so much of it that he became an expert on the subject; expert enough to write his book with chapters about chat shows, commercials, soap operas, game shows and so on, all peppered with evidence of his contempt: 'inane ... two-dimensionally bland ... television adores characterlessness ... monotony ... reduction of the viewer to morbid helplessness ...' and so on.

Worst of all for the future of the medium is the antagonism not of any particular professional group but of a seemingly large proportion of that band of people known as 'opinion formers': authors, journalists, critics, designers, playwrights, publishers, theatre and cinema producers, and so on. It is depressing to find that the very people who should be leading the way in bringing discrimination to the use of this new mass medium are still dismissing it lock, stock and barrel, largely – so far as one can tell – out of petulance at their own lack of will-power. Many are, of course, capable of considering television in a calm and unemotional way, but a quite extraordinary number seem incapable of any such reasoned approach. When in the spring of 1985 the Folio Society organized the first 'Literary Dinner and Debate' the motion was 'That television is the enemy of literature', an assertion which produced a deeply dispiriting array of virulent reactionism, folk mythology and Luddism.

In the end this debate is hardly worth the breath which is regularly expended upon it since it is obvious that nobody in television wants to hunt down and burn every last copy of Shakespeare's plays or Tolstoy's novels. At most television wants to exploit Shakespeare for its own ends just as Shakespeare exploited Holinshed and generations of writers and dramatists have parasitized one another, each leaving the original works on the shelf in their pristine state for later generations to turn to. Yet even Jonathan Miller, producer of some of the best versions of Shakespeare on television, has lent guarded support to those who oppose television's habit of adapting and exploiting as every other medium has adapted and exploited. In the MacTaggart Lecture at the 1983 Edinburgh Television Festival Miller expressed the belief that in putting Shakespeare on television 'some curious injury is done to the work in question', adding that although television had the virtue of introducing a large number of people to the plays, 'they return to the theatre now disappointed by the fact that the theatre does not live up to the pictorial glamour that television provided'.

This final point is unworthy of a man as intelligent as Miller, relying as it does on the old Mary Whitehouse technique of inventing a mythical 'they'. Just as Mrs Whitehouse claims that 'they' (which is to say we) are being seduced and corrupted by all the dirt and horror of television despite the fact that the effect upon herself of monitoring all the dirty bits is solely to turn her more and more firmly against them, so Miller similarly projects the failing on to us. Peter Conrad uses the same trick. The last paragraph of his book claims, 'We have almost been persuaded not to accredit the reality of anything unless we can experience it at second hand, mediated by the television cameras.' On the day that Mrs Whitehouse comes before us in sackcloth and ashes declaring that she has been corrupted by television, Miller declares not that 'they' are now disappointed in theatrical Shakespeare but that he is, and Conrad declares that he has been persuaded not to accredit the reality of anything unless he can experience it mediated by television, they may start to gain some credibility. Similarly writer Michael Holroyd will become more convincing on the day he alters his claim – 'Whatever moments of excellence it achieves, television is a natural enemy of the other arts and has almost overwhelmed them. It has taught us to be impatient. We almost want the pictures in galleries to *move*' – and substitutes 'me' and 'I' for the weasel words 'us' and 'we' thus making the claim sound as ludicrous as it really is.

Holroyd was the proposer of the motion in the Folio debate and he used all the standard ruses of the literary *ancien régime* to try to belittle and blacken television: the pathetic fallacy, the double standard, the appeal to puritanism, and so on. Writing on the subject previously, he had tumbled into the pathetic fallacy by asserting that television 'is not something we look at and control, but an eye that watches us and eventually controls the way we see ourselves' as though he really did believe like a two-year-old that television was magic and that the programmes were produced by mechanical rather than human means. In the debate he used the same sort of fey kiddy-science claiming that television's effect upon people was similar to its effect upon the magnetic strip on his plastic bank card which he left near the set: 'It looked as good as ever but the virtue had gone out of it.' Like the teacher who approved of her pupils reading *Beano*, Holroyd approved of reading because it was 'something requiring active participation' (like mugging, forgery and torture – are they too consequently desirable?).

Holroyd claimed that 'Most television people are not interested in words, they do not use them in the rigorous way employed by writers, they prefer to replace a writer's language with a bland telespeak.' Could he really be trying to tell us that Barbara Cartland

and Hank Janson, two writers who sell considerably more books than Holroyd, use words in a rigorous way, whereas Alan Bleasdale and William Trevor use bland telespeak? Of course not, it was merely another example of the old double-standard ploy in which you invite your listeners to compare the very worst aspects of the thing you dislike with the very best aspects of what you like: *Crossroads* compared to *Anna Karenina*, *Dempsey and Makepeace* compared to *Don Quixote* – isn't television awful? The trick works just as effectively the other way round, of course: while the modern electronic medium of television is providing millions of viewers with serious drama such as *Threads*, supremely informative series such as *The Living Planet* and deeply thoughtful works such as *Sea of Faith*, what is the disreputable old medium of print pumping out? *Penthouse* and *Playboy*, Mills & Boon romances, the *Sun* and *Daily Star*. Isn't print awful?

There is another type of unease which seems widespread among the folk of Acacia Avenue, closely connected to that techno-fear which expresses itself in defensive baby talk about anything scientific, and also closely connected to the guilt induced in those raised with the Protestant work ethic by anything that comes too easily: a fear that television is 'taking over', and living our lives for us. Old Etonian Michael Holroyd touched on it when he ridiculed television for its 'tendency to make us instantly well-informed about matters we know nothing about ... We travel without moving, we learn without very much thinking ... Everything comes easily.' This sort of objection makes a kind of sense if you come from a background where travel and books, serious conversation and expensive education are the norm: compared to such rich first-hand experience television must of course seem second-hand and second-rate.

But most people have no such background. It is an absurd upper-middle-class fantasy to imagine that if only people could be induced to turn their televisions off they would all start reading Solzhenitsyn and going to Covent Garden or attending lectures on the Late Renaissance. Most people deprived of their television pick up the *Sun* or listen to Radio 1. It is sometimes suggested that in the days before television 'took over' there was a golden age when families clustered around the piano and made their own entertainment; when voters participated in public meetings instead of being fed predigested political messages by the telly; when the railwayman and the factory worker rushed out after supper to attend WEA lectures and scampered home to read H. G. Wells. No doubt there were people like that. Yet even the crudest analysis suggests that the figures for people 'doing their own thing' – whether jogging or gardening, attending evening classes or ballroom dancing – have gone up during the television age and not down.

A memorable programme by Trevor Philpott looking at South African society just before the beginning of television there in 1976 showed that up to that time people were indeed obliged to make their own entertainment, even to the extent of clustering around the piano, and quite appalling it was too. One saw vividly what a godsend television is for most people. The continuing fuss about politics with frequent claims that elections have become merely television circuses, in which 'image' counts above all and policies not at all, looks like a classic proof of Hitler's dictum that the most successful lies are the big ones. Not only does television do a tremendous amount to publicize the issues in elections (certainly in Britain, anyway) to the extent that the electorate today is surely far better informed than in any previous age, but it also does what no other mass medium has ever been able to do: conveys a vivid impression of the personality and character of the politicians to every voter. Even during the greatest days of Gladstone's or Bevan's public meetings only a tiny minority of the population would have been able to see political leaders in the flesh, and in any case the belief that successful mob oratory is somehow a better qualification for high office than successful handling of an interview with Robin Day seems a most peculiar idea. In the sixties we were told that, thanks to television, no one who was old, fat or female would ever stand a chance of being elected to high office. Since then Ronald Reagan, Edward Heath and Margaret Thatcher have won five elections between them.

The vital question is: *why* do people like Holroyd feel so deeply hostile to television and why is his hostility greeted with such enthusiasm by the dinner-jacketed denizens of Acacia Avenue? Why was it that a phrase I heard at a Hampstead dinner party in 1954, 'We only have a television for the servants', had merely evolved by 1984 into a phrase overheard at another dinner party in Highgate, 'We only have a television for the au pair, it helps her with her English', without losing any of its self-satisfied overtones? And given that the 1984 speaker proved later in the evening with her criticisms of recent *Dallas* and *Dynasty* episodes and her detailed comparison of the styles of the current chat shows chaired by Michael Aspel, Michael Parkinson and Terry Wogan, to be an avid viewer of the more meretricious programmes, how should we explain such hypocrisy?

The answers surely lie in guilt and the nature of the television medium to date, and the solution could lie in the new technologies. Holroyd gave the game away when he admitted, 'I am, potentially at least, an addict ... I will watch anything rather than nothing; television gives out at night before I do.' The trouble is that with our present broadcast television services every owner of a television set is sent every programme willy-nilly. Whereas all the other media of expression offer the individual a choice – we choose which newspapers to buy, which books to read, which concerts to attend or records to purchase – television is wholly indiscriminate; every viewer is obliged to pay for everything (either via the shopping basket or the licence fee) and is then sent everything.

Of course it is still possible to exercise choice. With the schedules in the daily papers, and the channel selector switches, not to mention the 'Off' button, nobody is forced to watch programmes they do not want. But the weak will of most viewers and the seamless web in which one programme is joined to the next all too often ensure that even if we start out simply to watch the news or some other sensible item we rapidly find ourselves involved in a chat show or a situation comedy. It is like taking down *War and Peace* from the shelf and finding after one chapter that you are deep into *Killer's Payoff*. The result is that the inhabitants of Acacia Avenue who never see *Penthouse* or the *Cupid Rode Pillion* type of pulp romance, who never really experience the rubbish that makes up the bulk of the print medium (or the rubbish that makes up the bulk of music, or even the bulk of the performing arts which must consist of drag and strip shows), do become intimately aware of the rubbish on television. And then, like Mr Holroyd, they unload their guilt by pretending that television contains a higher proportion of rubbish than the other mass media and they blame television for their own weak will in watching it.

One solution is already to hand. The VCR allows you to record just those programmes which you really want to see and to watch them whenever you choose. Like other owners Mr Holroyd would no doubt find that acquiring a VCR can cut down your viewing time because the mere act of recording a programme often seems sufficient; once the programme is in your possession, available for viewing at your convenience, all sense of urgency about watching it tends to disappear. It is remarkable how few programmes really seem to need watching at all once they have been kept on the shelf for a few days. In the longer term the guilt and hostility of Holroyd and Acacia Avenue will surely be eased by systems of transmission and purchase – whether pay cable, scrambled DBS signal, or instant ordering of cassettes via interactive systems – which will allow the consumer the same degree of choice and control as currently exists in other media of expression.

CHAPTER THIRTEEN

If You Can't Beat 'Em, Join 'Em, Even If You Can't Find 'Em

Before coming to the pros and cons of the various futures suggested for British television, there is one ominous trend that should be considered now because it is with us already. The danger is that in response to what is seen as the threat of the new technologies, our existing television services will be altered, or worst of all will alter themselves, out of all recognition, transforming themselves into something awfully like the organizations against which they have been warning us. It would be bad enough to do that and become the harbinger of the very thing they oppose; worse still, or anyway more ironic, to do it and then discover that the threat never materialized, or not in the expected form. While cable and satellite were still no more than pie in the British sky there were already three groups seemingly intent upon making radical alterations to existing broadcasting structures: the broadcasters themselves, market-obsessed politicians, and those who would dearly like a few changes for their own benefit.

Most noticeable among this last group have been those arguing for the introduction of advertising to the BBC. So powerful has their voice been, and so receptive the Thatcher administration, that immediately after granting the 1985 licence fee increase the Government appointed yet another review body under Professor Alan Peacock to investigate the advisability of introducing advertising to the BBC and to advise on the likely effects upon other mass media if the step were taken. Not a few cynics within and without the BBC took it as a foregone conclusion that Peacock would declare in favour of the Corporation starting to take advertising, however gradually. So when news man Alan Protheroe was removed from the post of Assistant Director-General shortly after the committee's appointment and accountant Michael Checkland was dramatically promoted to the position of Deputy Director-General, this was interpreted as a determined BBC attempt to beef up its financial muscle in preparation for Peacock's examination. Before their committee had even had a chance to meet, let alone start reaching conclusions, the Thatcher Government had had the effect of significantly altering the balance of interests on the BBC Board of Management, reducing the programme-making interests in favour of accountancy.

For public consumption the reasoning of those who lobbied so vigorously for the Corporation to be turned over to commercials went something like this: in an age when cables and satellites make an irrelevance of the old scarce-wavelength argument for regulating broadcasting in the name of the greater public good, why should the BBC expect to continue being treated like some rare and delicate plant? Why should the BBC alone be protected from the harsh realities which affect other mass media whose success depends upon satisfying the public? If the *Daily Mirror* and the *Guardian* and the *Financial Times*, not to mention Granada Television and London Weekend and Border TV, can all exist in the market-place without needing a poll tax to support them, why should the BBC be entitled to one now that technology has given television a potential for diversity virtually as great as that of the print medium? If *Horizon* or *Omnibus* or *Panorama* appeal to so few people that those series cannot survive without the protection of such a tax, then what right do they have to exist at all?

It is an argument with a seductively rational appeal to those who would dearly like to see broadcasting breaking free from the shackles of regulation and taking its rightful place alongside print as an independent partner in the fourth estate, but it overlooks one crucial fact: technology has not yet given Britain that vaunted diversity. At the time of writing we do not have multi-channel broadband cable, or indeed any cable at all except the old upgraded systems, the small operation in Swindon and a few odds and ends in other cities. As yet the only satellite services are experimental and directed mainly at Europe. For the overwhelming majority of the population BBC1 and BBC2, ITV and C4 are the only services available. What is more, whereas it looked only a short time ago as though this would be changing quite quickly, it now looks as though we may have to wait years if not decades for cable and satellite to arrive. Today it is not entirely far-fetched to suggest (though I do not believe it) that cable and satellite may never have any great effect upon the UK but might be overtaken by some other, as yet undiscovered or undeveloped, technology.

It should anyway be borne in mind that while this respectable argument for pushing the BBC into the market-place is advanced in public, those who are most keen on such a change are the advertising people whose main motive is really the desire to break the ITV monopoly and thus reduce costs. In a similar vein it is worth noting that in 1985 during the public debate over the BBC licence fee and the Peat Marwick report on BBC finances and efficiency, two particular groups of newspapers were loudest and most insistent in their demands for change at the BBC, their suggestions ranging from the closing-down of the BBC's *Breakfast Time* to the breaking-up of BBC services and their auctioning to the highest bidder. The first group of papers was *The Times*, *Sunday Times*, *News of the World* and *Sun*, all owned by Rupert Murdoch, and the second group was the *Daily Express*, *Sunday Express* and *Daily Star*, all owned by Fleet Holdings. Fleet Holdings is the largest shareholder in TV-am, the ITV breakfast service which would stand to gain most from the closure of *Breakfast Time*, and Mr Murdoch is the owner of Sky Channel and a man with large ambitions for his own interests in the new television technologies. The special pleading went largely unidentified as such, though BBC Director-General Alasdair Milne was at one point heard to say: 'Who, I would like to ask, is more likely to serve the public interest: a broadcasting organization which is considered the world over as the leading producer of quality broadcast programmes, or *The Times* whose recommendations, if acted upon, would have the practical effect of enabling its owner, Mr Rupert Murdoch, to acquire some of the most valuable broadcasting action in the United Kingdom?'

But however dubious the special pleading from without, what was far more worrying was the change being wrought within the British broadcasting institutions. In the cynical phraseology of the soccer field both BBC and ITV looked as though they were 'getting in their retaliation early'. For example the BBC, determined to maintain and, as it hoped, increase its audience share in order to maintain its claim on the licence fee, launched in spring 1985 a season which built its BBC1 schedule on two helpings of soap opera and three chat shows a week. Some objected that this formula looked cynically and single-mindedly concerned not with quality or public service but with the maximizing of ratings; precisely the preoccupation which the BBC so strenuously condemns in its potential cable and satellite competitors. It is not that, however, or not primarily that, to which we should object. We certainly should complain about the rather mediocre quality of so many BBC programmes in the eighties: far too often in recent years (too often for the BBC's own good) it has been ITV which has set the trends and won the awards as well as commanding the biggest audiences. If the BBC is to sustain its special claim on the licence fee it must somehow boost its quality/popularity quotient. What is needed is a lot more of the flair which the BBC showed in the sixties when it first came out fighting for the popular audience. But in principle the BBC must be allowed to use one of its channels to maximize its audience, and the outcry which greeted the idea of switching *Play of the Month* from BBC1 to BBC2 during the same season was misplaced.

The old Reithian concept of broadcasting (of luring an audience into watching programmes which they would not readily choose by putting together a mixed schedule with light entertainment used as sugar coating to disguise the pills) is a trick which – apart from being a patronizing attempt at social engineering – just will not work in the new era of television. In the age of abundance inertia will not keep uninterested viewers watching *Antigone* on BBC1; they will zap across the other channels with their remote controls. Those who still maintain, as James Cellan Jones, the BBC's former Head of Plays, did when the channel switch was suggested, that 'It is part of the BBC's job to put on classical drama at peak times whether it attracts a large audience or not' (and he made it clear that he meant on BBC1) are just going to have to accept that BBC2 is now as widely available as BBC1 and that viewers must be allowed to choose for themselves.

Our concern should be to ensure that while the BBC fulfils its job of pleasing as many people as possible on BBC1, and does so with high-quality programmes, a combination it has frequently achieved in the past, it maintains and increases the proportion of more demanding material on BBC2. The danger is not that BBC2 will become a highbrow ghetto but that it won't. Many of the forces in the new technologies drive towards channel specialization, obvious examples being Ted Turner's all-news channel CNN and EMI's Music Box. This is not to say that mixed schedules will quickly die; that seems most unlikely. It is to say, however, that viewers in the future will increasingly want to know more or less what to expect when switching to a particular channel. The danger with the BBC is that having cleared the less popular programmes off BBC1 it will be tempted, if it still attracts too few viewers, to clear them off BBC2 as well, attempting with two popular channels to achieve the licence-justifying figures which it failed to manage with one. Were this to happen there would seem little point in continuing to champion the BBC; its claim on our loyalty is that it is special, and that it maintains a range from the most popular to the most demanding. So far, by the skin of its teeth, it has continued to command that loyalty.

Nor does the danger of our present broadcasting organizations becoming precisely what they fear concern only programmes. The BBC has also proved itself quite ready to fudge its own dearest principles in pursuing its policy of massive pre-emptive strikes. Having held itself determinedly aloof from commercial broadcasting for sixty years, the Corporation suddenly decided, it seems, that the only way to withstand the onslaught from commercial satellites was to get in there first. Having beaten ITV to the draw by going to the Government and laying claim to any rights which might be dished out to Britain under international satellite agreements (all the ITV companies and the IBA were completely preoccupied at the time with the renegotiation of ITV company licences and the bidding for breakfast television) the BBC was handed two satellite channels on a plate.

However, when it began to investigate the possibilities it found that the cost of building and launching satellites and running celestial services was prohibitive. Even that, however, was not enough to persuade it to give up the plan and admit that it might be a good idea to let a few modern merchant venturers take the risk and see whether they could fill a public want. Almost anything, it seemed, would be better than letting in those awful people who wanted to make money – even driving a massive wedge into your own principles. So, after years of opposition to commercial television, the BBC turned round and offered to climb into bed with the devil it knew, ITV, rather than risk the ravishment of some new devil. The result was the Satellite Broadcasting Board (SBB) manned by three Governors of the BBC and three Members of the IBA with the chairmanship alternating between the two organizations, Lord Thomson, Chairman of the IBA, being the first. In *Airwave* (Winter, 1984–5) he explained: 'For the first time in the history of British broadcasting, technological change has brought the IBA and the BBC together.' He went on to describe the co-operative satellite venture:

> The SBB will not be built in the same image as the IBA: it has a different job to do. Pay-to-view DBS must recognize the sovereignty of the consumer. It is a high-risk commercial venture that will stand or fall on its ability to attract subscribers, already paying a licence for their BBC channels and receiving the advertising-funded ITV channels. A market-based service must, to a significant degree, be regulated by the market.

Almost before those words appeared in print, serious doubts arose about whether the BBC/ITV satellite plans would ever get off the ground. But that does not affect the point being made: that the BBC was quite ready to go massively into debt with its bankers in order to join ITV in a 'high-risk commercial venture' which would 'to a significant degree be regulated by the market', and all in the name of forestalling commercial DBS. It puts one in mind of the American Army officer in Vietnam who said that in order to save the village his men had had to destroy it.

The BBC was not alone in these preparatory strikes against the so-far absent enemy. From about 1983–4, the more blatantly commercial sections of ITV began pressing the IBA to start 'de-regulating' their business, in other words slackening or abandoning the rules imposed on broadcasters. The evidence suggests they have had a remarkable amount of success.

Under the old IBA such moves would have been unthinkable. Up to 1980 the Chairman of the Authority was Lady Plowden, daughter of an admiral, former Vice-Chairman of the BBC, former Chairman of the Professional Classes Aid Council and the Working Ladies Guild, and blessed with the suitable Christian names of Bridget Horatia. Her Director-General was Sir Brian Young, son of Sir Mark Young. After education at Eton and King's College Cambridge, Young had been Headmaster of Charterhouse and there were some in the ITV companies who said that in spirit he never abandoned his gown and mortarboard. Putting your hand up and asking the IBA for a slackening of the rules while those two were in charge was a waste of time. But then Lord Thomson of Monifieth, former Labour MP George Thomson, became Chairman of the IBA, Young retired, and instead of the expected promotion internally of Colin Shaw (at that time Director of Television at the IBA, previously Chief Secretary at the BBC) John Whitney was brought in from outside. At this surprising move some of the more quick and pushy souls in the ITV companies rubbed their hands in glee.

Whitney they realized was educated not at Eton and King's but at Leighton Park Friends' School, Reading, which he left at sixteen. By the age of twenty-one he had formed a company to make advertising programmes for Radio Luxembourg and was running his first Rolls-Royce. Later he became one of the key members of the Local Radio Association, the group which lobbied strenuously and successfully for the introduction of commercial radio to Britain. By 1982 when he was invited to become Director-General of the IBA Whitney was Managing Director of the biggest and most prosperous commercial radio outfit in the country, London's pop station Capital Radio. On the way up he had also built a career in independent television and film production, being involved in such successes as *The Plane Makers*, *Upstairs Downstairs* and *The Flame Trees of Thika*, as well as a film called *The Buttercup Chain* which is described in Elkan Allan's *Guide to Movies on Television* as a 'dreadful semi-incestuous sex fantasy with Hywel Bennett, Jane Asher and others who should have known better'.

Thus he was a self-made man and very much of his time: he took up his post at the IBA in the middle of the first Thatcher administration just as the disciples of the market philosophy began to hit their stride. It seemed inevitable that the old schoolmasterly approach of the Authority towards its ITV wards was about to change, and sure enough there has been all sorts of slackening in the rules. It is another example of the way in which the prevailing political philosophy and the mere threat of the new technologies work together to produce considerable changes in our existing television structures. There has been relaxation in the rules governing sponsorship, the great American bogy which was produced so often as a frightener by the opponents of commercial television during the 1954 debate. The British were promised that spot advertising would be the only source of revenue permitted in this country, but in 1984–5 the rules were revised to allow companies to advertise in the commercial breaks in the middle of programmes covering events which they are sponsoring – a grandmother's-footsteps approach to full-blown American sponsorship. Another slackening of the rules in spring 1985 allowed brand names to be used on screen in acknowledgements to companies providing funds to support television programmes.

The Nelson-like blind eye which the IBA turned towards TV-am when it abandoned its contractual obligations in such an obvious and shameless manner after the farce of its opening weeks is seen by some as the clearest indication of the new spirit of indulgence towards the companies. But the most telling item of evidence was actually a speech made at the end of 1984 by a poacher turned gamekeeper: Michael Grade, the former ITV Programme Controller who joined the BBC to take control of BBC 1. Talking of what he called 'ITV's less fettered pursuit of the largest possible audience', he said, *inter alia*:

So many of the strict IBA rules which governed the ITV schedules seem to have gone by the board lately. These rules were designed and enforced by the IBA to reconcile the companies' honest commercial ambitions with the Authority's definition of what a full public service, albeit privately funded, should look like. If memory serves, ITV programme controllers used to be faced with what seemed like about sixty-nine scheduling 'do's and 'don't's ... The rules covered such areas as the suitability of material for family viewing. Example: all series and films had to be certificated by the companies and vetted by the officers of the Authority. The certification categories were: suitable any time, suitable after 7.30, after 9.00, or in exceptional circumstances after 10.00.

What do I find? *The A-Team* at six o'clock on Saturday. Here is a well-made US action series (which I certainly would have bought for the BBC) going out at an hour that would have been unthinkable three years ago. However wittily disguised, the show glories in the use of guns, guns, and more guns as the white hats triumph over the black hats. I wouldn't like to have to defend its placing so early. I remember the pained expression on my late and beloved LWT predecessor Cyril Bennett's face when he complained to me that the Authority had refused him permission, after a lengthy argument, to schedule *Hawaii Five-O* at 7.25 on Sunday after the closed religious period (the period ends at 7.15 these days) because the show was certificated post 7.30. The argument was about a slippage of just five minutes. *The A-Team* is scheduled an hour and a half earlier than used to be permissible. Let's take *The Professionals*, a popular home-grown action series, one that I commissioned myself. It was clearly a show for transmission after nine o'clock, yet those same episodes that in my day were post nine are now scheduled as repeats at 8.45. What are parents to make of the broadcasters' assertions about the nine o'clock family viewing watershed?

Let us take reward shows. The Authority's rule in my day used to be a limit of three in any one week, no more than two of them in peak time, and certainly it would have taken the persuasive talents of the Attorney-General to argue the case for having two on the same night. In the current issue of *TV Times* I counted no fewer than nine big-prize game shows on ITV including no fewer than three in tonight's schedule. The total value of cash and prizes on offer this week and most weeks this autumn I calculate at around £20,000. The prerequisite for IBA approval of these programme formats is that the game must include an element of skill. The only skill competitors seem to need is the skill to actually get on some of these shows as contestants...

Some years ago the IBA introduced a rule that prohibited centre-break advertising in designated children's programmes. It seemed to them to be undesirable for children to have their appetites whetted by ads for toys and bikes and things which their parents couldn't or wouldn't afford. I noticed watching the almost wall-to-wall children's output of TV-am's early Sunday morning that it was crammed with advertisements for toys and games and tempting Christmas goodies. This is not, of course, a point that illustrates any scheduling rule change. Nevertheless, taken with the points I have just made, it does serve as yet more evidence that ITV are now competing with a new relaxed rule book.

Take religion: the Sunday commitment to place half an hour of religious material outside the closed period (i.e. 6.40 to 7.15 where religious material is mandated on both channels) used to mean that ITV placed the admirable *Credo* and its equivalents around five o'clock when the available audience reaches peak-time proportions. ITV has now persuaded the IBA to let them slide this back to two o'clock against all the desires of the Central Religious Advisory Committee which watches over the two main channels. Again I offer no criticism, I just point out the significant softening of the rules.

It was clear, said Grade, that in view of their competitors' relaxation in the scheduling rules BBC 1 would have to adjust its strategies. Not long after, his channel duly launched a new wave of evening schedule starters: the soap opera *EastEnders* on two weekdays and the *Wogan* chat show on the other three. As in the late fifties it could, once again, be interpreted as an example of commercial competition forcing the BBC to move closer to the tastes of the majority of its audience. Provided *EastEnders* offers good and thoughtful popular drama (as ITV's *Coronation Street* often does) and provided *Wogan* offers good conversation there is not necessarily anything wrong with that, particularly if BBC2's schedule simultaneously starts to concentrate more on programmes for the more demanding viewer (which is a big 'if').

However, these various pieces of evidence taken together – the Corporation's lightening of its BBC1 programmes, the IBA's slackening of the controls on scheduling, the relaxation of sponsorship rules, the BBC's willingness to join ITV in a 'high-risk commercial venture' selling direct satellite broadcasts to those who can afford them, the blind eye turned to TV-am's failure to fulfil its contract – seem to suggest that long before any new competitors with fresh technologies arrive to turn British broadcasting into a true marketplace the BBC and ITV have already decided that they cannot beat them, so they will join them … even if they never arrive.

CHAPTER FOURTEEN

AD 2000 and the Birth of Television

To be fair it must be admitted that while cable and satellite may be slow in coming to Britain, our broadcasters are already facing increased competition for the viewer's attention. For our parents deciding what to watch on television was simple: they either watched BBC1, and solely in the evenings, or they watched nothing. For us the choice is already much wider: BBC1, BBC2, ITV, Channel 4, breakfast television, our own VCR recordings, or our video dealer's rented films. Moreover, thanks to convergence, we can also use our sets for the teletext services of Ceefax and Oracle ('teletext' being broadcast text services carried piggy-back on existing television signals, which is why they can only be seen when the transmitters are operating), and for viewdata services such as British Telecom's computerized data bank Prestel or the interactive Homelink scheme which already allows us to shop and bank from our sitting-rooms ('viewdata' being services which supply text and other material via cable at the demand of the individual user at any time, the cable employed by Prestel and Homelink being the telephone wire), or we can hitch a home computer to the television and play 'Dungeons and Dragons'. Thanks to this expansion it has become fashionable recently to talk about the arrival of the 'third age' of broadcasting. The suggestion is that the first age lasted from the birth of radio in 1922 until 1953 when the coronation gave that huge boost to television, and the second age from 1953 until the present, with the third age being marked by the coming of the new technologies and the consequent increase in the quantity of television available.

Posterity may perceive fewer detailed divisions. It could be that we are only just beginning to reach the end of what will be seen as the introduction to television's real history – and an oddly misleading introduction at that. Compared to a mass medium such as print, television is still very young; there are plenty of people around who can remember the BBC's first soot-and-whitewash transmissions from Alexandra Palace in 1936. It is possible that the new technologies will indeed mark the beginning of a new era, but perhaps our grandchildren will see this as the true start of television. It would not be entirely surprising if they considered the first fifty years, from 1936 to 1986, as a bizarre anomaly: a period when phenomenally large audiences – a third to a half of the entire UK population – frequently watched the same programme at the same time. This, they will learn, occurred because our only means of transmitting programmes during this early period was to 'broadcast' them through the atmosphere from high transmitter masts using rare wavelengths; a limitation which ensured that for the first half century the largest number of channel choices we ever had was four.

In terms of content and quality maybe our grandchildren will regard these fifty years as a golden age: a brief period quite without precedent (comparable, perhaps, only to the flowering of the Elizabethan theatre when audiences, even in terms of the smaller population, were on a much tinier scale) during which tens of millions of ordinary people ingested an astonishingly rich diet of drama written by men such as David Mercer, Dennis Potter, and William Trevor; documentary series such as *Civilisation*, *The Ascent of Man* and *The World at War*; eye-opening current affairs series such as *World in Action*, *Panorama* and *This Week* which for the first time regularly revealed the British population to itself; socially astute comedy series such as *Steptoe and Son*, *Till Death Us Do Part* and *Dad's Army* which were sometimes more revealing than the current affairs programmes; and highly successful book adaptations such as *The Forsyte Saga*,

The Pallisers and *Brideshead Revisited*. All this, our grandchildren will hear with incredulity, was provided for a tiny amount of money collected in the quaint form of a 'licence fee' costing, even in the system's fiftieth year, about half the daily cost of *The Times*, only 12p a day per household, and in the case of ITV costing nothing at all so far as most viewers could tell.

Looking around at the plethora of television on offer during the third millennium, and noting the meretricious nature of the programmes chosen by most viewers, some of our grandchildren will doubtless mourn the passing of this golden age, and the coming of their own age of abundance. Yet perhaps the historians among them will point out that a similar golden age, when high-mindedness seemed universal, marked the early days of print, and for much the same reasons: there was precious little choice – you read the Bible or a few other improving texts, or you read nothing.

Should we, then, accept an increasing flood of television as inevitable and resign ourselves to the arrival of an even bigger deluge of bland international pap? There are cynics who are already saying that that is precisely what we must do, but such gloom is absurd. It does indeed seem inevitable in the long term that the quantities of undemanding popular material on offer from television will grow and grow following the patterns set by print, food, music and so many other commodities. There is, however, no reason whatsoever why we should accept the self-serving line put out by the BBC that the only choice is their own schedule, which they consider so supremely worthy, or 'wall-to-wall *Dallas*'. The important thing to ensure is that as the total output of television expands, the proportion of high-quality material is maintained, so that although the dross may outweigh the gold by ever-increasing amounts, those of us who want it do still get more gold and not less: 5 per cent of 20 programmes may be easier to find in the schedules than 5 per cent of 200 programmes but the fact remains that the second arrangement does give you ten times as many good programmes.

As viewers what we should be demanding is that we keep the best of what we have got and add as many as possible of the advantages offered by the new technologies: greater choice, more specialization, an increasing shift of power from the broadcasters to the audience, greater convenience in timing and format – in other words more chance than ever before for most people to watch whatever they want whenever they want to. At this we can be sure that the members of the duopoly will smile pityingly and declare that we are being dreadfully naïve and cannot possibly have the best of the old and the best of the new but that we must protect them from the ravages of the approaching revolution or risk losing all we now have. At that we must stand our ground, refuse to be browbeaten or blackmailed, and remind them that the BBC adopted exactly the same expression of deep conviction in 1954 when warning us all just as convincingly of the holocaust to come. They regarded ITV then as the bubonic plague, yet today they see ITV as brothers in arms, so admirable that they are quite willing to go into business with them to run DBS services.

The attitude towards the new age of television among the members of the present duopoly often looks like panic: 'Oh dear! Oh dear!' they twitter. 'The goths and the vandals are coming with their cables and satellites! Save us, save us, or everything good in television will be lost and everything bad will replace it!' It is absolutely true that some of the forces driving towards satellite television and cable systems have much to do with audience maximization, and that some of the early 'narrowcasting' applications of cable have failed in the US. But it is also true that off-air broadcasting is as much concerned with audience maximization as any other system; that DBS could offer a high-quality/high-cost system of a sort that could never be run off transmitter masts; and that while there will of course be failures in an infant industry such as cable, this particular technology offers more hope of fine targeting and individual choice than any other television system yet devised.

It also seems peculiarly cynical, not to say unrealistic, to imagine that, unlike every other medium of expression and mass communication, the new television technologies will be peopled exclusively by philistines. No doubt philistines will be numerous just as they are in popular music, popular publishing and popular food, but no doubt there will also be people like those who started Granada TV or Penguin Books or Sainsbury's whose aims are popularity *and* quality. America's twenty-four-hour news channel CNN supplied by the brash newcomer Ted Turner is a remarkable and, in many ways, excellent service (even if he does rely upon non-union journalists to keep costs down). In Italy Silvio Berlusconi, who created the most successful of the *de facto* national networks, clearly felt deeply that his operation was regarded as something of a 'pirate' business and as soon as the Government hinted that his operation might be legitimized he started planning a prestige news programme modelled on CBS's excellent *Sixty Minutes*. Said Berlusconi: 'The times of juke-box TV are over. We are now a television service true and proper, entrusted with the essential brief of any authentic broad-caster; to keep abreast of events and to transmit news of them to the entire nation.' His desire for respectability could result in many Italians finally getting what they have so long wanted: a high-quality television news programme. Reiner Moritz, the most experienced deal-maker and co-producer in Anglo/European arts programmes, has often said that if only the technicians will give him access to a pan-European satellite he will be delighted to promote pay-per-view opera.

As viewers we should oppose the destruction of the existing British television system which seems to satisfy the audience to a very large extent. This is evident both from the way that the British use their VCRs for time-shifting (watching more television rather than switching away from television to watch rented movies) and from successive opinion polls. For example the Consumers' Association survey 'TV and the Future: The Viewers' View' published in February 1984 showed that 81 per cent of people were very satisfied or fairly satisfied with BBC1, 69 per cent with BBC2 and 67 per cent with ITV. Channel 4 scored only 18 per cent but that has presumably changed since. Only 3 per cent derived little or no satisfaction from any channel.

Experience over a number of years in talking to groups ranging from young schoolchildren to old age pensioners suggests that even though the licence fee is regarded by some as forbidding, very few would want to economize by doing away with less popular programmes, even those they personally never watch. There is an endearingly proprietorial pride about what is perceived as the BBC's wide choice and high quality. It is commonplace to hear people say, 'No I don't watch that sort of thing myself but my sister/friend/son does.' Though they may very rarely watch *Horizon* or *Newsnight* or *Shakespeare* a remarkable number of people seem to take satisfaction and even comfort from the fact that such series are there when wanted.

Suggestions that the BBC should be forced to take advertising are premature; time enough for that when it really does look as though market forces are bringing us the greatly increased diversity which we have so often been promised. When that occurs it will by definition become impossible to continue the peculiarly British system of a duopoly, and the BBC will simply have to change, as it has with consistent success on many previous occasions. But until that time, and it may be much longer coming than some entrepreneurs would wish, we would be insane to start dismantling or radically altering the Corporation, or indeed the ITV system. For all its faults – its almost unvarying commitment to the status quo, the consequent narrowness of the views it represents, its disregard (except on Channel 4) for independent voices, its nationalism and parochialism – the duopoly has proved itself over thirty years: it pleases the bulk of the British public to an extent which is very rare in any other sphere of endeavour, and in the international sphere it proves its superiority over and over again.

In practical terms the major difficulty has been the growing discrepancy between ITV and BBC incomes with steadily increasing advertising revenue on one side and ever greater demands on the licence fee on the other side. The events of 1984–5 blurred this picture somewhat; ITV's rising income graph suddenly flattened out and the BBC, although not given anything like the increase it wanted, did receive a rise of 26 per cent in the licence fee. One day, as the technological revolution comes really close to home, it could be that the BBC and ITV will feel they have so much more in common with one another than with their competitors that outright co-operation between the two old rivals will make sense; they already share transmitter sites, some advisory committees, certain events such as the Royal Command Performance, and so on. What is more, Granada sometimes seems rather better than the Corporation itself at preserving BBC traditions and standards. Come the millennium it would not be so surprising to find ITV bailing out the BBC in order to preserve the power of the duopoly for a little longer in the face of new competition.

In the meantime the BBC's greatest need is to find a way of collecting income invisibly as ITV does. There is a widespread belief that ITV is 'free', as though the people who run Anglia or Scottish TV were kindly paying for it out of their piggy banks. In fact, of course, we all pay for ITV just as surely as we pay for the BBC, though by collecting through the shopping basket the ITV system is slightly more equitable in taking most from the rich, who spend most, and least from the poor, who spend least. One of the objections to the licence fee is that it is 'regressive', weighing heaviest on the poor. The BBC has always claimed that it makes programmes more cheaply than ITV and no doubt this is true, one of the reasons being that the unions treat the Corporation more gently than the commercial companies. But it is always immensely difficult to establish precisely what ITV programmes do cost, and how much the cost of advertising loads on to prices in the shops. Raymond Snoddy of the *Financial Times* reported on this subject for the BBC programme *Did You See?* in the spring of 1985 and wrote in *The Listener* afterwards:

The advertising research organization MEAL tried to work out the cost of television advertising on a range of household products for *Did You See?* According to MEAL, after removing factors such as airtime discounts and advertising agency commissions, the percentage of the price of products accounted for by television advertising ranges from 0.33 per cent for a car to 14.65 per cent on baby-care products. On a shopping basket of goods costing £6.20 *Did You See?* estimates the cost of TV advertising was 31p. On a box of disposable nappies costing £3.25 the present cost of TV advertising accounts for 47p.

It is often asserted that despite such figures commercial television really is free in effect because advertising leads to increased sales and consequent economies of scale so that products cost us less than they otherwise would. But it is hard to believe that UK consumption of detergent goes up enough year after year to go on making this true; easier to believe the evidence of our eyes: that much if not most television advertising aims to make us switch brands, not increase our consumption. What the BBC needs most in all the world – more than a new Broadcasting House, more than a successful soap opera – is a means of revenue collection which is as inconspicuous as ITV's. Though we pay more for ITV nobody ever complains; it is the size of the BBC's lump sum which offends politicians and pensioners alike. Since television is powered by electricity the answer could be a percentage on electricity bills; it would be less regressive than the licence fee and much less noticeable. If the BBC does not come up with something of this sort then its relationship with successive governments will inevitably get more and more difficult and its standing *vis-à-vis* ITV less and less impressive.

It is symptomatic of the guilt felt about television in Hampstead, Oxford and a thousand Acacia Avenues that whenever the introduction of new technologies such as cable and DBS is mentioned, reactions there are almost invariably hostile and pessimistic. 'Is there any evidence that people actually *want* satellite television?' they ask. The answer of course is that there is not, just as there was no evidence that people actually wanted horseless carriages before they were offered them. If public clamour for fresh inventions were the criterion nothing would ever change: imagine going around in 1949 asking people 'Do you want a reel of transparent plastic tape with gum on one side?' or 'Would you like a new pen with a ball-bearing instead of a nib? – You'll have to throw away the whole thing when the ink runs out.' You would have been dismissed as crazy, but who today would be without ballpoints or Sellotape? 'Don't you think we have quite enough television already?' people ask. 'After all there's far more than one person can possibly watch.' By the same reasoning we should have stopped writing books and composing music long ago.

Thanks to the vested interests of the British broadcasting establishment we have heard at length about what they see as the dangers of de-regulation and the depredations they believe would follow. Much less has been heard about the danger that, owing to a mixture of hostility from the British broadcasting establishment, ineptitude among politicians, timidity from British investors, and conservatism among the broadcasting unions, the public will be denied the advantages of the new technologies and new forms of television for many years. In the long term this danger would probably lead to a greater foreign influence in British broadcasting than ever before as overseas satellite operators (not only American but those operating off the European and Irish satellites with footprints covering most or even all of Britain) moved in to fill the void.

As viewers we are faced with the delicate task of attempting to get our political and broadcasting representatives to avoid all these dangers: not to allow the BBC and ITV to turn themselves into precisely what they fear in others; not to allow the innate conservatism of so many British institutions to withhold from us the benefits of the new technologies; and not to allow sudden de-regulation to wreck the valuable compromise of the duopoly. It is worth remembering that it was not pressure for programme excellence in the first place which brought us the two organizations which formed the duopoly: the BBC grew out of a band of wireless manufacturers, and ITV was formed by impresarios, industrialists and journalists. In neither case was the production of a high-quality programme schedule the first or main driving force behind their initiative. The coming of the BBC resulted from the arrival of a new technology and the coming of ITV resulted from commercial opportunism.

More new technologies and more commercial opportunities are now in prospect. The thing to do is keep our heads, and keep the duopoly (which means, as viewers, being willing to pay and even champion the licence fee; a willingness only doubted by a few neurotic politicians) until market forces really do bring diversity. Some time after that, government control of broadcasting will begin to look just as appalling as the control of printing by Star Chamber. But we could well reach the year 2000 before it happens.

Index